THE
KIRKYARD OF
COWIE
ST. MARY OF THE STORMS

ACKNOWLEDGEMENTS

My thanks go to colleagues Margaret Brown and to Jim & Jean Shirer for the original work on this graveyard. Marjorie & Sandy Edward completed the cross-check and special thanks must go to Sandy for his excellent plan of the first extension. Edna Cromarty dealt with the final queries before it headed for the publishers. Edna also did the index and wishes to thank Jean for help with checking this.

Because of the huge number of entries for the surnames Christie, Lees & Masson, a request had been made by the Society Research Team when it was still in draft form in the Shop for a breakdown index for these surnames. This we have compiled and we trust it will be helpful.

The graveyard and chapel remains are on a very ancient site. There is a most interesting information board at the entrance as well as some fascinating stones in the cemetery - well worth a visit even for those not so interested in family history.

In loving memory of HENRY WILLIAM BAYLY who fell asleep 7 Jan.1904 aged 58.

(Square on the ground) In memory of WILLIAM GEORGE CURRIE d.3 Dec.1900 aged 3 also MARY DANIEL CURRIE d.2 Jan.1905 aged 3.

1791. WN. CR. In memory of WILLIAM NEIPER (sic) late tenant in Blackhills d.20 Oct.1791 aged 64; their children MARGARET, JEAN & WILLIAM.

1790. GB. MB. In memory of GEORGE BUCHAN in Cookney d.1 Apr.1801 aged 81; MARY BEATTIE his wife d.14 Oct.1793 aged 65. Their children WILLIAM BUCHAN son to GEORGE BUCHAN in Burnside of Maryculter d.30 June 1789 aged 21; JOHN & EUPHEMIA d.in infancy. (Back) GB. MC. In memory of GEORGE BUCHAN tenant in Cookney & elder of this parish d.13 Apr.1816 aged 61 also ANDREW BUCHAN his son d.15 Jan.1790 aged 8 and MARGARET COLLIE his wife d.10 Apr.1836 aged 78.

Sacred to the memory of GEORGE BUCHAN d.Cookney 18 Feb.1842 aged 51; his wife CHRISTIAN BUCHAN d.6 June 1861 aged 75. GEORGE BUCHAN was son of ANDREW BUCHAN shipmaster in Aberdeen & nephew to the late GEORGE BUCHAN farmer Cookney.

1866. Erected by CATHARINE WATT Windford, Muchalls in memory of her husband WILLIAM SPARK d.5 Sept.1853 aged 45. Said CATHARINE WATT d.Mill of Uras 9 May 1902 aged 91. Their children JAMES d.1842 aged 2; JANE d.1843 aged 5; WILLIAM d.19 Jan. 1866 aged 31; CHRISTINA d.7 Nov.1869 aged 24; ANDREW d.20 Aug.1911 aged 69.

1826. In memory of JAMES SPARK d.28 Apr.1856 aged 82; JANE LYON his wife d.5 Mar.1867 aged 92. WILLIAM son of JAMES SPARK wright at Kingcausie d.11 Jan.1825 aged 17 also JOSEPH d.9 Apr.1839 aged 25. ROBERT d.17 Jan.1843 aged 34; MARGARET youngest dau.of above b.13 May 1817 - d.14 Dec.1909 aged 92.

JS. IM. In loving memory of JAMES SPARK farmer Cantlohills d.27 July 1901 aged 84; his wife ISABELLA MESTON d.27 Aug.1911 aged 77. Their son DAVID BURNETT SPARK d.25 Apr. 1878 aged 3 weeks 4 days.

1841. JS. JS. To the memory of JOSEPH SPARK d.Cantlohills 10 Aug.1868 aged 93; JANE SPARK his wife d.10 Nov.1862 aged 84. GEORGE son of JOSEPH farmer Cantlohills d.22 Feb.1841 aged 30; his son JOHN d.23 Sept.1849 aged 38; his dau.JEAN d.11 June 1857 aged 50 & JOSEPH d.7 Apr.1878 aged 64. MARGARET d.13 Mar.1891 aged 82 & ALEXANDER d.11 Feb.1899 aged 79. 4 lines text.

To the memory of JOHN SPARK late farmer in Hillocks, Muchalls d.in 1820 aged 48; ANN KNOWLES his wife d.in 1851 aged 77. ALEXANDER their son d.in 1849 aged 33. JOHN SPARK tenant in Hillocks d.29 Nov.1873 aged 74; their dau.ANN d.15 Mar.1891 aged 80. JAMES SPARK tenant in Hillocks d.1 June 1897 aged 84.

In memory of JEAN SPARK wife of ALEXANDER FOWLER d.5 May 1861 aged 85; said ALEXANDER FOWLER d.17 May 1861 aged 75.

Sacred to the memory of GEORGE KNOWLES blacksmith Stonehaven d.1845; his wife MARY SPARK d.11 Sept.1868. Their family MARY d.young; ANN d.30 Sept.1849; KEITH d.15 Dec. 1871, MARGARET d.9 Nov.1896.

13 1832. JP. MP. In memory of JAMES PITHIE once wheel wright in Crag of Newhall d.9 Dec.1820 aged 75; MARGARET PYPER his wife d.4 June 1831 aged 71. Their children ANNE d. in infancy; their son-in-law WILLIAM STRATHDEE d.1 Dec.1847 aged 51; JANE PITHIE his wife d.22 July 1875 aged 79.

---

14 Erected by AGNES E.D.MORGAN in loving memory of her husband GEORGE CHRISTIE d.31 July 1916 aged 41; said AGNES E.D.MORGAN d.15 Jan.1955 aged 82.

---

15 Erected by WILLIAM TAYLOR Newtonhill in memory of his children JOHN d.4 Jan.1860; CATHERINE d.2 Mar.1876; CHARLES d.22 Feb.1885. His wife ELIZABETH MILNE d.3 Feb. 1905 aged 67. Said WILLIAM TAYLOR d.23 Sept.1910 aged 78; his dau.MARGARET d.25 Jan. 1922 aged 51.

---

16 (Heart) In memory of JAMES D.SIM aged 5mths. 1906.

---

17 Erected by ISABELLA BREBNER in memory of her husband ALEXANDER ALLAN merchant Stonehaven d.8 June 1862 aged 66. Said ISABELLA BREBNER d.12 Apr.1877 aged 86. 2 lines text.

---

18 JR. HT. To the memory of JOHN ROBERTSON once tenant in Upper Mount-gate-head d.18 Oct. 1848 aged 47 & HELEN THOMSON his wife d.6 May 1895 aged 85. ANN their dau.d.31 Jan.1852 aged 8.

---

19 To the memory of GEORGE STOTT farmer Greenheads, Muchalls d.11 June 1851 aged 47; his wife ISABELLA WATT d.7 May 1886 aged 82. Their son JOHN STOTT farmer Powburn, Laurencekirk d.30 Dec.1896 aged 56; ELIZABETH MASSIE his widow d.Laurencekirk 5 Aug.1912 aged 73.

---

20 Erected by JANE MASSON in loving memory of her husband ALEXANDER LAW d.12 Aug.1915 aged 73; above JANE MASSON d.18 Oct.1934 aged 93.

---

21 Erected by ALEXANDER SIM farmer Allochie in memory of his son ALEXANDER d.25 Feb.1879 aged 5; his dau.CHRISTINA ISABELLA ANN d.22 Mar.1889 aged 17 mths. The above ALEXANDER SIM d.Tillyhowes, Banchory Devenick 14 Sept.1915 aged 85; HELEN THOMSON his wife d.Hillside, Banchory Devenick 10 Apr.1940 aged 90. Their dau.ELIZA TURRIFF d.20 Dec. 1960 aged 68.

---

22 Face gone.

---

23 Erected by WILLIAM MAIN fisherman Stonehaven & MARY CHRISTIE his wife in loving memory of their children MARGARET ANN d.26 Nov.1891 aged 3 weeks; WILLIAM d.6 Jan.1895 aged 3mths. Above MARY CHRISTIE d.1 Nov.1920 aged 51; above WILLIAM MAIN (latterly harbour-master) d.17 Dec.1925 aged 58.

---

24 1856. Erected by JOHN WATTERS mason Well Head, Muchalls to the memory of his only dau. MARY ANN d.5 Oct.1850 aged 13. Above JOHN WATTERS d.25 Feb.1891 aged 77; MARGARET MARTIN his wife d.30 Dec.1892 aged 80.

---

25 1858. Erected by THOMAS ABERDEIN in memory of his dau.JANE d.28 June 1848 in 5th year; son JAMES accidentally drowned at the Chincea Islands 28 Jan.1866 aged 19. MARGARET LONGMUIR his wife d.24 Mar.1870 aged 48.

1848. GS. HW. In memory of GEORGE SPARK wright Cantlohills d.1 Apr.1859 aged 90 &
HELLEN WYLLIE his wife d.1 Sept.1822 aged 41. Their son JOHN d.17 Apr.1848 aged 33.
CHRISTINA COLLIE his 2nd wife d.27 Mar.1857 aged 72. (Back) 1804. JS. MG. To the memory
of JOHN SPARK wright in Cantlohills d.6 Mar.1821 aged 83 also, MARGARET GERDEN (sic) his
spouse d.8 May 1803 aged 60. Likewise MARGARET SPARK their dau. d.21 Apr.1816 aged 31.
Also MARGARET their dau. d.in infancy.

Erected by DAVID DURWARD farmer Drumhendry in memory of his wife JANE SPARK d.12
Mar.1898 aged 79. Their sons WILLIAM d.6 Aug.1875 aged 24; DAVID d.18 Mar.1878 aged 31;
ALEXANDER killed at Herriot, New Zealand 10 Apr.1893 aged 39. Said DAVID DURWARD d.29
Sept.1903 aged 85; MARGARET d.11 Nov.1924.

1850. FORBES & CATHARINE MILNE Kirkland in memory of their children ANDREW d.20 Oct.
1837 aged 4; CATHARINE d.2 Nov.1838 aged 3mths; GEORGE d.11 July 1839 aged 3; FORBES
d.21 June 1849 aged 19. Above FORBES MILNE d.26 June 1860 aged 63; above CATHARINE
MILNE d.7 Nov.1882 aged 82.

(Flat) JE. IL. Here lyes the children of JOHN EDWARD in Chapiltoun of Elsick viz. JOHN d.25
Aprile 1732 aged 5, MARGRET d.25 Feb.1734 aged one year.   1735.

1837. In memory of JOHN DAVIDSON gardner (sic) in Stonehaven d.17 Sept.1836 aged 86 &
CHRISTIAN BURNETT his 1st wife d.15 Mar.1796 aged 37. Their son GEORGE d.in infancy.
CATHRINE DICKSON his 2nd wife d.in Apr.1829 aged 54. Their dau. MARGARET d.30 Nov.
1835 aged 26 & CHRISTIAN d.in infancy.

1787. JD. MM. In memory of JOHN DICKSON gardener in Cowie d.22 Apr.1804 aged 68 &
MARGARET MANZIE (sic) his spouse d.11 Dec.1811 aged 72. Their son DAVID d.17 Feb.1796
aged 21. SUSAN DICKSON dau. to JOHN DICKSON d.19 July 1786 aged 14. ELISABETH &
ELSPET d.in infancy. JEAN DICKSON spouse of JAMES HALL d.14 May 1808 aged 29.

Erected to the memory of CHRISTINA LEES wife of ROBERT MASSON d.18 Jan.1949 aged 60;
above ROBERT MASSON d.15 Mar.1974 aged 84.

Erected by CHRISTINA CHRISTIE in memory of her husband ANDREW LEES d.6 Apr.1928 aged
71. Her son THOMAS d.24 Apr.1887 aged 7mths. Above CHRISTINA CHRISTIE d.11 Aug.1930
aged 67. (Heart) THOMAS LEES aged 7mths.

Erected by JAMES LONGMUIR & MARGARET PITHIE in memory of their family: MARY d.28
Apr.1842 aged 19, JAMES d.26 Oct.1853 aged 24, ROBERT d.17 Mar.1854 aged 16, DAVID d.5
July 1860 aged 29. Above JAMES LONGMUIR late blacksmith at Hillside d.19 Nov.1873 aged 83;
MARGARET PITHIE his wife d.9 Mar.1875 aged 76. ANN LONGMUIR d.14 Aug.1900 aged 73;
CHARLES LONGMUIR d.27 Oct.1907 aged 63. (Back:) 9 lines verse.

(Large piece of the face out of the middle) AA. EM. In memory of ALEX(ANDER AND)ERSON
who d............il 1886/ag.................rs/E..............R/who di.................1893/ag........rs/G..........DIE/
who d............. ed 36/and MARY.......TON his wife d.3......ember 1854 aged 73 also/ MARY
GIBSON d.in infancy. MARY MOIR neice (sic) of ELLENAR MOIR d.1 Mar.1914 aged 74. (Face
now completely gone)

----

36   1860. Erected by ALEXANDER BLACK merchant Hill of Muchalls to the memory of ANN
      BROWN his wife d.1 Jan.1860 aged 26.

      Erected by ALEXANDER MAIN fishcurer Sketraw in memory of his wife JANET MASSON d.21
37   Mar.1879 aged 48; said ALEXANDER MAIN d.10 Dec.1899 aged 60. His dau. JANET d.23 Apr.
      1912 aged 43 - interred at Hitcham.

      1857. Erected by JAMES FRASER wool spinner Stonehaven & JANET WOOD his wife in memory
      of their children JAMES d.3 June 1852 in infancy; ISOBELLA d.26 Oct.1856 aged 3yrs 6mths.;
      THOMASINA SCOTT d.27 Apr.1862 aged 3yrs 6mths.; ANNIE d.11 Aug.1866 aged 2yrs 2mths.;
38   JOHN W. THOMSON d.30 Mar.1871 aged 7mths,; ROBINA d.30 Aug.1874 aged 8; ROBERT W.
      d.14 Dec.1875 aged 9mths. Above JANET WOOD mother of the family d.26 May 1887 aged 52;
      above JAMES FRASER d.10 Jan.1890 aged 66. Bottom: Also ISOBELLA ROBERTSON d.16 June
      1881 aged 93.

      JR. IE. Here lies JAMES ROBERTSON late tenant in Balquharan d.16 Dec.1746 aged 81 also
39   ISOBLE EDWART his spouse d.6 Feb.1772 aged 95. Here lies MARGARET ROBERTSON dau.to
      JAMES ROBERTSON tenant in Balquharan d.12 Feb.1754 aged 39. (Spellings as on Stone)

      Erected by public subscription to the memories of 4 of the crew of the Stonehaven life-boat
      "St.George" viz.JAMES LEIPER coxswain, JOHN BROWN assistant coxswain, ALEXANDER
40   MAIN & JAMES LEES who were drowned while endeavouring to enter Aberdeen Harbour after
      an attempt to render assistance to the "Grace Darling" of Blyth 27 Feb.1874. JAMES LEIPER is
      interred in Belhelvie Churchyard, ALEXANDER MAIN in Nigg Churchyard, JOHN BROWN &
      JAMES LEES are buried here.

      Erected by JAMES MILNE in memory of his father JAMES MILNE merchant Skateraw d.16 Jan.
41   1841 aged 56; his mother ANN CHALMERS d.9 Feb.1858 aged 58. His brother GEORGE d.12 Dec
      1839 aged 3½.

      (Table) [To the memory of?] WILLIAM MARNOCH farmer in Quoch...? d 19 Mar.1806? aged 8-.
      And ISOBEL ROBERTSON his spouse d.30 Dec.1779 aged --. And of their children ALEXANDER
42   & KATHARINE d.in infancy. This stone was erected by WILLIAM MARNOCH their son. Also the
      above named WILLIAM MARNOCH late tenant Woodside of Elsick d.10 Oct.1832 aged 72 also his
      spouse CATHERINE BISSET d.14 June 1840 aged 85.

      1878. Erected by JOHN MASSON & ELIZABETH MASSON his wife Skaterow to the memory of
      the said JOHN MASSON d.18 Nov.1904 aged 66 & ELIZABETH MASSON his wife d.25 July 1916
43   aged 69. Also JOHN their son d.31 Aug.1878 aged 8 & ISABELLA their dau. d.25 Aug.1947 aged
      68. Their oldest son JAMES fisherman Skateraw d.23 May 1957 aged 89; his wife ISABELLA
      CHRISTIE d.24 Mar.1960 aged 85. Their son JAMES d.24 Feb.1976 aged 77.

      Erected by JOSEPH CHRISTIE & ANN MASSON in memory of their dau.MARY d.5 Aug.1878
      aged 5 years 7mths.; their son JOSEPH ALEXANDER d.8 Jan.1883 aged 14 mths.; dau. ISABELLA
44   MASSON d.5 Mar.1884 aged 4yrs. 9mths.; son GEORGE d.12 June 1884 aged 4mths.; dau.ANN
      d.24 Apr.1888 aged 7mths. Above ANN MASSON d.6 Nov.1900 aged 52; above JOSEPH
      CHRISTIE d.24 Mar.1904 aged 56.

      Erected by ANDREW MAIN fisherman Stonehaven in memory of his family WILLIAM JOSEPH
45   d.11 Feb.1875 aged 4 mths.; HENRY JAMES d.6 Feb.1886 aged 14mths.; ALEXANDER d.18 Feb.

/1886 aged 21. ANN d.4 Mar.1903 aged 35; MARGARET d.12 July 1908 aged 38. Said ANDREW
MAIN d.26 Apr.1913 aged 76; MARGARET LEES his wife d.27 Aug.1928 aged 86. 2 lines text.

In memory of ISABELLA MELDRUM midwife, for many years resident at Stranathro, Muchalls d.
there 3 Feb.1875 aged 89. Text. This stone was erected by many friends in grateful remembrance
of constant & disinterested kindness to the poor; of genuine honesty & simplicity of character and
of great professional skill evinced throughout a long & useful life.

Erected by JANE CRAIG in memory of her beloved husband ROBERT CHRISTIE fisherman
Skaterow d.16 Nov.1895 aged 70; son JOSEPH d.1864 aged 1. Said JANE CRAIG d.7 Aug.1899
aged 80. MARGARET WOOD wife of JAMES CHRISTIE d.30 Mar.1899 aged 42; said JAMES
CHRISTIE d.11 Sept.1927 aged 75. Verse.

Erected by WILLIAM CHRISTIE & MARY BRODIE Sketraw. Here rests the body of their dau.
MARY d.24 Apr.1872 aged 2 also a 2nd MARY d.19 June 1875 in infancy. Above WILLIAM
CHRISTIE d.5 Apr.1918 aged 78; MARY BRODIE d.9 Sept.1920 aged 80. (Space) In loving
memory of JOHN CHRISTIE son of JAMES & MARGARET CHRISTIE d.29 Nov.1889 aged
3mths. Said JAMES CHRISTIE was drowned at sea 120 miles from Aberdeen 15 Sept.1901 aged 37.
1 line motto. Also the children of WILLIAM & ANNIE CHRISTIE: HELEN ANN d.25 Jan.1899
aged 4 and MARY d.26 Jan.1899 aged 24 days. Also JOHN son of above WILLIAM CHRISTIE &
MARY BRODIE lost at sea with the *"Golden Sceptre"* 29 Jan.1937 aged 55. 2 lines text. (Back)
Also in loving memory of HELEN dau. of WILLIAM CHRISTIE & MARY BRODIE d.16 Mar.1949
aged 71; her sister ISABELLA d.14 Apr.1959 aged 76. ALEXANDER son of above HELEN d.16
June 1978 aged 77. A prince among men. Also his wife MILDRED CHRISTIE 1889 - 1987.

(Cross) In loving memory of our dau. NELLIE wife of LAWRENCE LINTON.

Erected by JAMES CHRISTIE fisherman Torry & JESSIE BRODIE his wife in loving memory of
their dau. MARY d.9 Mar.1901 aged 10mths.; their dau.NELLIE wife of LAURENCE (sic) LINTON
d.23 Jan.1928 aged 31. Above JESSIE BRODIE d.21 Nov.1934 aged 66; above JAMES CHRISTIE
d.31 Jan.1948 aged 79. 5 lines verse.

Erected to the memory of GEORGE BROWN Upper Cairnhill d.10 Apr.1888 aged 72; JANE
LONGMUIR his wife d.11 May 1887 aged 61. Their dau.ANN d.3 July 1924 aged 66; JEAN d.21
Feb.1927 aged 77.

Erected by JOHN BROWN tenant in Mid-Fiddes, Drumlithie in memory of his wife JANET
WALLACE d.30 Dec.1866 aged 41. Their children SUSAN d.7 Apr.1860 aged 7; JAMES d.2 Oct.
1861 aged 3; CHARLES THOMSON d.5 Oct.1861 aged 7. Said JOHN BROWN d.11 Oct.1876 aged
59. JOHN d.14 May 1880 aged 33. Bottom: JAMES TAYLOR BROWN son of JOHN BROWN
Junr. Mid-Fiddes d.4 Sept.1898 aged 18.

1835.WB. CH. In memory of WILLIAM BROWN late tenant in Upper Cairnhill d.23 Sept.1851
aged 73; CHRISTIAN HUNTER wife of WILLIAM BROWN tenant in Upper Cairnhill of Elsick
d.12 Nov.1834 aged 55. Their dau.ISABELLA BROWN d.2 Nov.1882 aged 71.

Erected in memory of WILLIAM BROWN farmer Upper Cairnhill d.Sunnyside, Maryculter 17 Dec.
1888 aged 75; his wife ISABELLA THOMSON d.20 Nov.1898 aged 85. Their daus. ISABELLA d.
in 1865 aged 20; JANE d.7 Jan.1927 aged 73; ANN d.8 Oct.1927 aged 80.

55
Erected by JAMES & MARGARET CHRISTIE Sketraw in loving memory of their family
ALEXANDER 4th Gordons fell in action at Arras 10 Apr.1917 aged 19; ANDREW d.5 July 1889
aged 3; MAGGIE d.12 June 1894 aged 1. Above MARGARET CHRISTIE d.12 Feb.1934 aged 70.
Above JAMES CHRISTIE d.24 Apr.1943 aged 84.

56
1815? In memory of ISOBEL BRO(WN spouse to ROBERT) ABERCROMBIE Mo..... Arduthie
d........ 1813 aged 28 & JAMES their (son) d.Apr.1813 aged 4. (Most now gone)

57
1778. TB. MM. Here lyes MARGRAT MILLNE (sic) late spouse to THOMAS BROWN late
tennant in Maggry d.22 Apr.1778 aged 63.

58
1863. TB. MS. In memory of THOMAS BROWN late tenant in Burnorachie d.6 Mar.1863 aged 60
MARY SPARK his wife d.19 June 1866 aged 60. Dau. ELSPET d.13 Dec.1925 aged 90.

59
AK. JB. Erected by ALEXANDER KNOWLES Greenreas, Muchalls in memory of his son
THOMAS d.12 Jan.1885 aged 7yrs. 7mths. Said ALEXANDER KNOWLES d.Hillocks 8 Dec.1915
aged 75; JANE BROWN his wife d.24 June 1920 aged 78; their son JOHN d.25 Dec.1934 aged 55.

60
1778. DB. MM. And the afternamed DAVID BROWN d.17 Feb.1802 aged 92; his spouse
MARGARET MILNE d.22 Mar.1786 aged 70. Here lyes ye bodies of 4 children of DAVID
BROWNs tennant in Intown of Mountquich: JOHN d.28 Dec.1752 aged 13; JAMES d.15 Apr.1767
aged 25; ISABEL d.25 Nov.1769 aged 19 and DAVID d.15 June 1777 aged 33.

61
1840. In memory of WILLIAM BEVERLY late tenant in Quocies d.23 May 1839 aged 72; his wife
BARBARA BROWN d.25 Sept.1827 aged 60. Daus. ANN d.21 Nov.1817 aged 18; ELSPIT d.19
Feb.1861 aged 50. Son WILLIAM d.17 Jan.1871 aged 75. (Back) 1801. WB. JB. To the memory
of WILLIAM BROWN late indwellar in Uper Carenhill d.6 Jan.1805 aged 69; JEAN BURNES his
spouse d.7 June 1814 aged 78. Their children WILLIAM d.21 Dec.1770 aged 5; WILLIAM d.21 Jan
1783 aged 11; DAVID d.28 Nov.1800 aged 26. (Spellings as on stone)

62
1839. In memory of WILLIAM BROWN who was 51 years tenant on Burnside of Rickerton, 27 yrs.
an Elder of this parish d.10 Apr.1868 aged 74. EUPHEMIA TAYLOR his wife d.10 Nov.1878 aged
84. Their family WILLIAM d.27 Jan.1833 aged 7mths.; CATHERINE d.3 Mar.1871 aged 35;
CHRISTINA d.4 July 1882 aged 53. JOHN farmer Peattie & East Cairnbeg d.6 Feb.1892 aged 66,
interred in Fordoun Churchyard. ANN wife of ROBT. REID farmer Blairton, Belhelvie d.18 Dec.
1893 aged 63 - interred Allenvale Cemetery. MARY wife of GEORGE JAMIESON farmer Burnside
d.17 Jan.1909 aged 69; said GEORGE JAMIESON d.21 May 1927 aged 88.

63
WB. EB. In memory of WILLIAM BROWN late tenant in Hay, Park of Elsick, Elder of this Parish
for 23 years d.Burnside of Intown 12 Aug.1816 aged 58; his wife ELSPET BEVERLY d.11 Oct.184
aged 84. (Back) 1794. GB. IB. To the memory of GEORGE BROWN late tenant in South Mains o
Elsick d.15 May 1793 aged 78; his spouse JEAN BISSOT (sic) d.16 Dec.1812 aged 84.

64
1799. In memory of GEORGE CHALMERS d.Finlayston 2 July 17.. aged 50. CHRISTIAN
GARDEN his wife d.24 Nov.1796 aged 59. Renewed by ELISABETH CHALMERS their youngest
dau. in 1839.

65
Erected by ALEXANDER WALKER tenant in Blackhills of Cowie in memory of his wife ISABEL
SMITH d.19 Apr.1881 aged 64; said ALEXANDER WALKER d.26 Jan.1893 aged 81. Son-in-law
JAMES EDDIE tenant in Blackhills of Cowie d.Stonehaven 6 Dec.1908 aged 71; MARY WALKER

ont./his wife d.10 Sept.1911 aged 69.

In memory of our children MARY & SYDNEY.

Erected by ALEXANDER EDDIE in memory of his wife MARGARET DONALD d.1 Oct.1897 aged 25; said ALEXANDER EDDIE d.Canada 30 Sept.1934 aged 69.

1779. PC. IM. In memory of PATRICK CAIRD late subtenant in Wadieshillock d.3 July 1763 aged 40; Likewise JEAN MOUAT his spouse d.4 Jan.1790 aged 74. Their son JOHN d.11 Dec.1778 aged 24; ISOBELL d.in infancy; also their dau. JEAN d.11 June 1781 aged 34.

(Flat) Erected by WILLIAM DONALD Hillhead, Cowie in memory of his dau. MARY JANE d.1 July 1906 aged 25; son JOHN d.in infancy. Said WILLIAM DONALD d.4 Sept.1919 aged 84; his wife MARGARET COUTTS d.18 Mar.1930 aged 82. Eldest son WILLIAM d.21 Feb.1942 aged 72.

1806. JE. MM. To the memory of JAMES ETTERSHANK late tenant in Readyks d.29 Nov.1812 aged 69. Their dau.MARGRET d.7 Mar.1805 aged 23.

Erected by MARGARET LEES in loving memory of her husband JOHN CHRISTIE d.Torry 5 Jan. 1917 aged 52. JAMES their son d.23 Aug.1907 aged 5½. Above MARGARET LEES d.18 Sept.1952 aged 83. Bottom: Text.

1849. Erected by WILLIAM MASSON tenant Hilton in memory of his wife SUSAN WALKER d.16 Dec.1848 aged 47. Their dau.JEAN d.20 Aug.1848 aged 18, their son JAMES d.22 May 1844 aged 7. Above WILLIAM MASSON d.26 Oct.1873 aged 80. (Heart on Square in front) In loving memory of JOSEPH MASSON d.15 Apr.1903 aged 38.

In loving memory of WILLIAM MASSON tenant in Mill of Uras d.7 Mar.1888 aged 59; his wife MARGARET SPARK d.9 Oct.1913 aged 80. Of their family: GEORGE d.14 Sept.1874 aged 4mths., CHRISTINA d.18 Jan.1903 aged 30 & her husband WILLIAM SIMPSON d.28 Dec.1902 aged 30 - both are interred in Pittenweem Churchyard, Fife. WILLIAM d.9 Nov.1913 aged 54, ANDREW d.Temple, Kinneff 16 Mar.1924 aged 45 & ISABELLA PYPER his wife d.20 Feb.1945. MAGGIE HOUSTON d.1 June 1986. 2 lines text.

1800. AM. AM. This stone was erected by ANN MASSON in memory of her husband ANDREW MASSON late tenant in Raedykes d.11 Mar.1798 aged 58; above ANN MASSON d.24 Nov.1846 aged 86.

Sacred to the memory of ANDREW PATERSON turner Glaslaw d.9 Nov.1864 aged 50; his wife ANN BAIN d.New Brunswick. Their children ISOBEL & JANE d.in infancy. ANDREW husband of ELIZA PATERSON d.18 Feb.1918 aged 78; said ELIZA PATERSON d.8 Feb.1920 aged 76.

In memory of WILLIAM PATERSON once tenant in Croals Hillock d.8 Dec.1840 aged 77; his wife CHRISTINA MACKIE d.2 Sept.1855 aged 91. Their family ANDREW d.18 Jan.1872 aged 66, MARY BISSET d.26 July 1884 aged 83, WILLIAM d.6 Apr.1889 aged 86, his wife MARGARET MASSON d.12 Oct.1845 aged 43. Their son WILLIAM d.in infancy 2 June 1838.

1797. WP. MD. To the memory of WILLIAM PATERSON late tenant in Brounthillok (sic) d.9 Jan.1810 aged 82; MARY DOUGLAS his spouse d.8 Mar.1810 aged 72. Their children MARY PATERSON dau. Brounthillok d.10 Oct.1789 in 21st year, ALEXR. d.29 Sept.1793 in 18th year./

77cont./ Also JAMES d.16 Mar.1794 in 24th year.

----

78 Erected to the memory of ELIZA JANE HARRIS d.12 Rodney St., Stonehaven 19 Feb.1951 aged 82.
Her husband JOSEPH MASSON d.Brewlaw, Catterline 15 Apr.1903 aged 38. Their son Pte.
JOSEPH MASSON A.I.F. d.of wounds Gibraltar 20 May 1915 aged 23.

----

79 1855. JP. JK. To the memory of JOSEPH PATERSON farmer Haypark of Elsick d.12 Mar.1852
aged 77; JANE KEITH his wife d.16 Jan.1878 aged 91. Their children GEORGE d.26 Oct.1845 aged
19, WILLIAM d.19 Mar.1847 aged 23, ANDREW d.4 Mar.1849 aged 29. JOSEPH PATERSON
farmer in Chapelton of Elsick d.3 Sept.1856 aged 34. (Back) To the memory of JANE CHRISTIE
wife of JAMES PATERSON Tenant in Stoneyhill d.31 July 1867 aged 41. JANE their dau.d.4 Mar.
1870 aged 17, JOSEPH their son d.1 Mar.1871 aged 21; JAMES d.13 Feb.1873 aged 18. Above
JAMES PATERSON d.6 Jan.1875 aged 46. His 2nd wife MARGARET McDONALD d.29 May
1899 aged 83. WILLIAM their son, husband of JANE GORDON d.25 Mar.1936 aged 76.

----

80 PR. JW. In memory of PETER ROBERTSON once tenant in Whinshin, Megray d.20 June 1820
aged 93; JEAN WEBSTER his wife d.3 Feb.1806 aged 70. Their children PETER feuar Stonehaven
d.9 May 1855 aged 87, JAMES shoemaker Stonehaven d.4 Jan.1847 aged 77.

----

81 In memory of JEANIE C. ROBERTSON wife of JOHN S. MURISON Belmont d.7 Nov.1862 aged
26. HARRIET ROBERTSON 2nd dau.of PETER ROBERTSON merchant Stonehaven d.19 Nov.
1844 aged 3½. PETER ROBERTSON merchant Stonehaven d.3 Oct.1870 aged 62; HARRIET
WILKIE GLEGG his wife d.18 Dec.1879 aged 63.

----

82 In loving memory of ALEX. & ISABELLA.

----

83 Erected by WILLIAM CHRISTIE fisherman Skaterow in loving memory of his wife CHRISTINA
LEES d.13 Oct.1884 aged 24; son GEORGE d.13 Nov.1882 aged 7 weeks, dau.MARY JANE d.in
infancy in 1902. Son ALEXANDER husband of JEAN CHRISTIE d.11 June 1926 aged 27. Above
WILLIAM CHRISTIE husband of HELEN LEES d.19 Sept.1936 aged 76; above HELEN LEES d.9
June 1944 in 83rd year. 4 lines verse.

----

84 In memory of ROBERT SMITH once tenant in Blackhills d.26 Dec.1809 aged 73; JANET
GERRARD his spouse d.30 Dec.1820 aged 86. Their children AGNES d.1 Jan.1841 aged 77,
ISABEL d.8 May 1854 aged 84, GEORGE & ANN d.in infancy. (Back) In memory of ANDREW
SMITH tenant Blackhills d.16 Mar.1854 aged 82, ISABEL WOOD his wife d.19 Feb.1843 aged 67.
Their children ROBERT d.24 July 1818 aged 11, ISABEL d.in infancy, ANN d...........

----

85 1787. RS. KA. In memory of ROBERT SMITH weaver d.6 Mar.1821 aged 82; CATHERINE
AIRTH his wife d.19 Dec.1829 aged 93. Their sons JOHN SMITH d.Burnorrachie 6 May 1787 aged
23, WILLIAM d.2 Nov.1832 aged 63. CATHERINE their dau. d.3 Dec.1847 aged 70.

----

86 JF. EC. Here lyes JOHN FREEMAN seaman in Sketraw & husband to ELSPET CRYSTIE d.16
May 1752 aged 35; his spouse ELSPET CRYSTIE d.1 May 1772 aged 55.

----

87 Face gone.

----

88 In loving memory of JOHN TAYLOR fisherman, Cowie d.24 Dec.1863 aged 43; ANN LEES his
wife d.12 Apr.1852 aged 25. Their family: JAMES d.7 Aug.1867 aged 19, JOHN d.26 Jan.1884 aged
31, CHRISTINA d.in infancy, ANN d.6 Feb.1930 aged 81.

1844. In memory of JAMES TAYLOR late seaman in Cowie d.28 Feb.1843 aged 61. Their sons JAMES d.at sea 8 Mar.1831 aged 19, ANDREW d.7 Aug.1830/1? aged 13.

(Most gone) ....aged 68. ALEXANDER their son d.5 Nov.1782 aged 7.

Erected by ALEXANDER TAYLOR in loving memory of his family MARTHA d.10 Mar.1867 aged 10mths., MARGARET d.16 Feb.1868 aged 6 weeks, MARTHA d.26 June 1881 aged 1mths.,JESSIE d.3 Apr.1884 aged 8. Above ALEXANDER TAYLOR d.29 May 1927 in 85th year; his wife MARTHA DAVIDSON d.13 Apr.1929 in 85th year.

AN. EF. Here lyes ANDREW NEPER son to ANDREW NEPER seaman in Sketraw d.3 June 1743 aged 34.

In loving memory of JEAN TAYLOR d.3 Sept.1939 aged 67; her neice (sic) ANNIE E.HAMPTON 'DAISY' d.15 Aug.1922 aged 19. ANDREW TAYLOR husband of the above JEAN TAYLOR d.6 Apr.1944 aged 85. ALEXINA 'VIOLET' MACKIE d.13 Jan.1983 aged 74, sister of DAISY & ROBERT HAMPTON. 2 lines verse.

Erected by JESSIE REID in memory of her husband JOHN GRANT farmer North Hilton, Netherley d.8 Oct.1887 aged 65. Said JESSIE REID d.Aberdeen 1 Aug.1924 aged 86. Their family: GEORGE d.13 Feb.1874 aged 21 days.

Erected by HELEN MAIN in memory of her husband ALEXANDER CHRISTIE fisherman, Muchalls d.1 Apr.1881 aged 78; said HELEN MAIN d.8 May 1885 aged 83. Their son-in-law JAMES LEES d.17 Dec.1905 aged 81; MARGARET CHRISTIE his wife d.21 Apr.1919 aged 91.

Erected by WILLIAM MAIN in loving memory of his wife JESSIE CHRISTIE d.2 Feb.1926 aged 84; said WILLIAM MAIN d.17 Sept.1926 aged 83.

1839. Erected in memory of JAMES LYON late farmer Craigwells of Neitherlay (sic) d.10 Dec. 1848 aged 78; JEAN BROWN his wife d.10 Feb.1863 aged 71. Their children ELSPET d.5 June 1824 aged 2, HELEN d.21 Sept.1837 aged 22, ELIZA d.28 Sept.1838 aged 18, JAMES d.17 Aug. 1839 aged 23. (Back) In memory of the children of JAMES LYON: MARGARET d.3 July 1845 aged 27, DAVID d.24 June 1847 aged 13, JEAN d.26 Mar.1852 aged 25, ANDREW d.19 May 1853 aged 28, ANN d.23 Apr.1860 aged 29.

Text. Erected by JANET CHRISTIE in memory of her husband DAVID TAYLOR d.31 May 1868 aged 48; dau. ISABELLA d.22 Mar.1862 aged 2. Said JANET CHRISTIE d.18 Jan.1904 aged 75. Son ROBERT TAYLOR d.19 Sept.1900 aged 48, his wife MARY WATT d.25 Mar.1912 aged 56.

1793. AF. MC. In memory of ALEXANDER FREEMAN late seaman Sketraw d.22 Feb.1793 aged 82; MARGARET CRAIG his wife d.22 May 1802 aged 87. Their children ISABEL, MARGARET, JOHN & ALEXR, he d.22 Mar.1791 aged 38, his dau. HELLEN d.in infancie.

Erected by JOHN & MARY TAYLOR Cowie in memory of their children MARY d.20 Apr.1851 aged 6, JOHN d.2 Feb.1852 aged 5, ROBERT d.7 Feb.1860 aged 10mths., JANE d.3 Jan.1864 aged 14, ELISABETH d.14 Dec.1866 aged 15, ALEXANDER d.3 Jan.1867 aged 14. Said MARY TAYLOR d.29 Apr.1870 aged 51; said JOHN TAYLOR d.18 Dec.1890 aged 75. Also in memory of JAMES TAYLOR 1/7th Gordon Highlanders fell in action in France 11 Oct.1916 aged 22, son of JAMES TAYLOR fisherman. 2 lines verse. ALEXANDER TAYLOR d.23 May 1931 aged 35. 1/

100 cont.	/line verse. Said JAMES TAYLOR fisherman d.26 Sept.1934 aged 79; MARY JANE MASSON his wife d.17 Sept.1942 aged 80. (In front) ALEXANDER CHRISTIE in loving memory. JEAN

101	In loving memory of our father & mother ROBERT TAYLOR d.1 Sept.1944, ELEANOR TAYLOR d.5 Aug.1945. 1 line text. (In front) Son ROBERT d.26 Sept.1975 husband of JESSIE FORBES d.30 Mar.1985.

102	In loving memory of our father ALEXANDER HARPER d.7 Aug.1923 aged 59, mother MARGARET JANE TAYLOR d.12 Nov.1949 aged 77. Daus. KATHLEEN d.1 Jan.1972 aged 62, MARTHA d.18 June 1975 aged 63, ELEANOR d.13 Nov.1994 aged 86.

103	In memory of SUSANNA BOADEN wife of ALEXANDER WATT Muchalls d.24 Mar.1869 aged 64; said ALEXANDER WATT innkeeper Muchalls d.5 Jan.1872 aged 67. Their son WILLIAM WATT postmaster Muchalls d.10 Mar.1912 aged 76.

104	Here lies the body of ALEXANDER NEPER late seaman in Cowie d.17 Sept.1780 aged 41; his spouse MARGRAT MASSON d.22 Feb.1777 aged 78. (Back) 1729. JN. AN. MM. Here lyes JOHN NEPER son to ALEXANDER NEPER seaman in Couie d.26 Aug.1726 aged 6.

105	Erected by ALEXANDER NICOLSON baker Stonehaven & ELIZABETH REID in memory of their children MARGARET d.20 July 1851 aged 4, JOHN d.4 Sept.1863 aged 28, ALEXANDER who was lost on a voyage from Malabrigo to England in 1874 aged 36. Above ELIZABETH REID d.13 Mar.1877 aged 66; above ALEXANDER NICOLSON d.25 Jan.1884 aged 72. WILLIAM d.31 Mar. 1891 aged 36.

106	To the memory of ANDREW (NICOLSON?) Wheelwright in Stonehaven d.27 Mar.182? aged 66. And of their children JOHN........(too far down to dig further)

107	To the memory of WILLIAM KILGOUR an original genius who exercised the craft of weaver at Glithnow for the long period of 62 years in the same house d.12 Mar.1837 at the advanced age of 86 By his friends. 4 lines verse.

108	In loving memory of JOHN PARGITER b.23 Jan.1815 - d.27 Oct.1879; CHRISTIAN ROBERTSON his wife b.7 Apr.1811 - d.12 Jan.1885. Their son ALEXANDER b.21 Sept.1847 - d.7 Oct.1913 at New York. Daus. MARY b.25 July 1845 - d.16 Jan.1915, MORIA (sic) wife of CHARLES RICKARDS b.2 Sept.1849 - d.10 June 1893.

109	1793. In memory of WILLIAM EDWARD lived in Waird of Auchollie d.27 Dec.1779 aged 55; his wife JEAN DUTHIE d.30 Nov.1776 aged 45. Their children ALEXANDER, ROBERT & JEAN.

110	In memory of DAVID DURWARD MOIR farmer Allochie d.28 Apr.1950 aged 79; his wife HARRIET GILL d.25 July 1926 aged 39. Their son THOMAS JOHN d.24 Sept.1928 aged 15.

111	In loving memory of GEORGE MOIR of Newbigging d.16 Apr.1923 aged 86; ELIZABETH DURWARD his wife d.24 Sept.1929 aged 87. Their family HENRY COOK d.Winnipeg 15 Feb. 1920 aged 34; WILLIAM, MARY & CHRISTINA d.in childhood, SARAH MARGARET d.26 Apr. 1958 aged 80, ISABELLA JANE d.9 Aug.1961 aged 90. (Now face down)

112	Erected by GEORGE BROWN Hillside of Portlethen in memory of his parents WILLIAM BROWN d.18 May 1860 aged 86; CATHERINE BROWN his wife d.7 Mar.1862 aged 78 & WILLIAM their/

on./son d.1 June 1813 aged 4.

(Very worn) In memory of JAMES MILNE wright Ca........hill d.1 Apr.185? aged 85 also JANET? BROWN his spouse d.2 Dec.1839 aged 67. (Back) 1805. NM. MG. This monument was erected in memory of NATHANIEL MILNE late tenant in Croalshillock d.9 Mar.1784 aged 52 also MARGARET GIBBON his spouse d.20 Dec.1799 aged 66.

WM. JC. To the memory of WILLIAM MILNE blacksmith at Windyedge d.7 Jan.1854 aged 49 & JANE CUSHNIE his wife d.23 Mar.1889 aged 82.

1812. In memory of JAMES STRACHAN blacksmith d.28 Dec.1842 aged 75 & ELIZABETH ROBERT spouse of JAMES STRACHAN blacksmith in Woodhead of Ury d.16 May 1811 aged 42. JAMES their son d.in infancy, JANE STRACHAN d.Stonehaven 17 Apr.1845 aged 70.

In memory of ALEXANDER STRACHAN d.Blackhill, Dunnottar 18 Dec.1878 aged 75; his wife ELIZABETH ROBERTS STRACHAN d.Stonehaven 12 Sept.1893 aged 81. (Back) 1795. JS. KT. To the memory of JAMES STRACHAN late tenant in Glithnow d.11 May 1780 aged 67; KETHARINE (sic) TAIT his spouse d.26 Nov.1795 aged 63. Of their children ALEXANDER d.28 Mar.1797 aged 23.

Erected by JAMES CHRISTIE in loving memory of his wife MARY CRAIG d.20 Mar.1904 aged 82 & of their children ANDREW d.8 Apr.1868 aged 22, HELEN d.27 Aug.1868 aged 9. Above JAMES CHRISTIE d.17 Apr.1905 aged 84.

1789. RG. JS. In memory of ROBERT GALLAWA late tennant in Southpark of Arduthie d.6 Aug. 1804 aged 85; JEAN STRACHAN the wife of ROBERT GALLAWA d.19 Nov.1788 aged 60. Bottom: And JAMES their son who d.in infancy.

(Table) 1797. JJ. ED. In memory of JAMES JAMIESON once tennant in Mounthamoc of Durres d.24 Dec.1796 aged 58. Also his spouse ELSPET DUTHIE d.23 Nov.1803 aged 58. And of their children GEORGE JAMIESON d.23 Dec.1796 aged 20, RECHAL who d.in Infency. Also their son JAMES d.in Holland Sept.1799 aged 27, John d.15 Sept.1800 aged 28. (Heart) In loving memory of CATHERINE J.JAMIESON d.1 Nov.1881 aged 4mths. (All spellings as on stone)

Erected in memory of JAMES JAMIESON late wright at Craggiecat d.12 Aug.1876 aged 63; ISABELLA WYLLIE his wife d.16 Mar.1889 aged 73 & their children JAMES d.1 Nov.1847 aged 10, GEORGE d.10 Jan.1857 aged 2, JANE d.1 May 1864 aged 21. Their grandchildren ANNIE LOW d.4 Apr.1874 aged 20mths.,WILLIAM & ANDREW d.in infancy also ANDREW d.17 Oct. 1887 aged 5yrs 3mths. PHILIP GILBERT 1843 - 1927. Bottom: Also MARY JAMIESON wife of PHILIP GILBERT d.3 Sept.1880 aged 36.

Erected by DAVID HARPER Stonehaven to the memory of HUGH HARPER his father d.in Apr. 1852 aged 78; ISABEL NAPIER his wife d.12 Apr.1861 aged 74. Their children HUGH d.in June 1851 aged 38, JOHN d.20 May 1865 aged 48. Said DAVID HARPER for 33 years sexton here d.2 Jan.1903 aged 80. (Back) In memory of CHRISTINA HARPER wife of JAMES MILNE Stonehaven d.27 Mar.1877   aged 61. JOHN their son d.19 Sept.1859 aged 8. Above JAMES MILNE d.25 Aug.1891 aged 76. CHRISTINA MILNE or BAIN their dau.d.25 Nov.1928 aged 75.

Here lies JAMES NAPIER son to JOHN NAPIER d.17 Dec.1733 aged 21. MARGRET NAPIER dep.8 June 1733 aged 12. (Back) JN. JA. 1727. JANET ABERNETHIE spouse to JOHN NAPIER

122cont./d.3 Feb.1734 aged 53. ELISABETH NAPIER dau.of JOHN NAPIER d.8 Jan.1727 aged 19.

Erected by GEORGE CHRISTIE in memory of his wife JANE MAIN d.2 Feb.1910 aged 41; son
123   WILLIAM killed in France 14 Nov.1916 aged 20; his dau.JESSIE d.17 Feb.1909 aged 6mths. Above
GEORGE CHRISTIE d.10 May 1942 aged 76.

1767. CO. HA. Here lies CHARLES ORCHIE late subtenant in Nether Carnhill d.28 Jan.1766
124   aged 88 also HELLEN ABERNETHY his spouse d.27 Jan.1760 aged 81. Likewise 6 of their children
and CHRISTIAN ORCHIE late spouse to JOHN MEASON in Greenhead d.21 May 1779 aged 72.

Erected by ALEXANDER CHRISTIE fisherman Stonehaven in loving memory of his wife MARY
125   MASSON d.1 Aug.1883 aged 39; said ALEXANDER CHRISTIE d.2 July 1914 aged 70. Their
family: MARY d.17 Sept.1881 aged 4mths.

Erected by his widow & family in memory of EDWARD ROBERTSON farmer South Cookney d.4
126   Mar.1913 aged 79; his widow ELIZABETH MAIN d.4 June 1926 aged 85. Their dau. ISABELLA
d.24 Feb.1957 aged 88; their son JAMES d.1 June 1958 aged 86. JAMES ROBERTSON d.3 Jan.
1944 aged 52.
----

127   Sacred to the memory of our mother JANE CHRISTIE wife of ALEXANDER MAIN d.Edinburgh
13 Jan.1930 aged 74; our father ALEXANDER MAIN d.12 Apr.1940 aged 83. 1 line text.

Erected by WILLIAM CUSHNIE in memory of his parents WILLIAM CUSHNIE d.8 Feb.1924 aged
128   84, BARBARA MILNE d.9 Mar.1927 aged 88. His sisters JEAN aged 2, ELSIE aged 5, BARBARA
aged 15.

(Table) To the memory of RYMOND STEWART a black man, a native of Grenada who lived for 30
129   years in the service of the late Mr FARQUHARSON of Breda in this County and was much
respected. He d.at Elsick 3 Jan.1834 leaving money which he had saved for charitable purposes.
----

130   In loving memory of ELIZABETH ISABEL TAYLOR d.9 Feb.1981 aged 70, wife of CHARLES
JAMES CARNEGY d.9 Feb.1986 aged 81. 1 line text.
----

131   In memory of WILLIAM ANGUS grain merchant Stonehaven (a native of Old Deer) and for many
years in the service of the proprietors of Raemoir & Cowie d.29 Jan.1923 aged 85.

Erected by ELSIE LEIPER in memory of her husband ALEXANDER MASSON d.6 Apr.1899 aged
132   42. Their family: ELSIE d.15 Apr.1894 aged 14, WILLIAM, HELEN, ELSIE & ROBERT d.in
infancy. Above ELSIE LEIPER d.31 Oct.1935 aged 80.
----

133   Face gone. (Shield behind) In loving memory of ALEXANDER CHALMERS d.25 Aug.1893 aged
28.

Erected by MARGARET CHRISTIE in memory of her husband JAMES PITHIE shoemaker Craig of
134   Newhall d.11 June 1861 aged 60. Above MARGARET CHRISTIE d.Muchalls 8 Mar.1894 aged 78.
Bottom: 4 lines verse.

Sacred to the memory of WILLIAM ROBERTSON wright Sketrawhead d.16 Apr.1845 aged 33; his
135   spouse SUSAN CHRISTIE d.8 May 1844 aged 33. CHRISTINA YOUNG wife of WILLIAM
ROBERTSON d.5 Mar.1875 aged 25. ELSPET R.ROBERTSON d.20 July 1875 aged 37. Said/

/WILLIAM ROBERTSON shoemaker d.19 May 1884 aged 44. Their sons WILLIAM d.3 Mar.1888 aged 17, JOHN d.21 June 1904 aged 23.

Erected by WILLIAM CHRISTIE & MARGARET BRODIE his wife in loving memory of their dau. MAY d.11 Jan.1910 aged 8. Their son WILLIAM d.7 July 1900 aged 3mths. Said MARGARET BRODIE d.16 Mar.1923 aged 57; said WILLIAM CHRISTIE d.2 Sept.1943 aged 79. Their dau. MARGARET JANE d.13 Mar.1967 aged 81 & her husband WILLIAM CHRISTIE d.28 Sept.1967 aged 82. Their son FRANK d.on active service 2 Oct.1942. Bottom: 4 lines verse.

ER. To the memory of JAMES ROBERTSON weaver Swinecrois d.1 Jan.1828 aged 76; JANE CROMAR his wife d.in Aug.1839 aged 78. ALEXANDER ROBERTSON crofter Cookney d.31 Jan. 1874 aged 77; JANE EDWARDS his wife d.4 June 1884 aged 85. Of their children ALEXANDER d.5 July 1854 aged 29, WILLIAM d.in June 1862 aged 39, MARGARET d.18 Nov.1898 aged 70.

Erected by ANN MAIN in loving memory of her husband ROBERT ADAM d.30 Apr.1904 aged 56. Their son ROBERT d.15 Apr.1882 aged 2. Above ANN MAIN d.1 Dec.1934 aged 82. (Heart in front) In loving memory of ISABELLA IRVINE TAYLOR wife of JAMES BAIN d.Stonehaven 4 Aug.1894 aged 60.

Erected by GEORGE ADAMS fisherman Stonehaven in memory of his wife JEAN CLARK d.8 May 1908 aged 68. Their son ROBERT C.ADAMS schoolmaster d.4 July 1911 aged 35, their dau.MARY ANN d.in infancy. Their son GEORGE d.at sea 20 Jan.1882 aged 20 - interred in Catterline Churchyard. Above GEORGE ADAMS d.20 Jan.1920 aged 87. Bottom: Motto.

In memory of GEORGE ADAMS d.Stonehaven 17 Feb.1880 aged 74; his wife ELSPET CHRISTIE d.Crawton 15 Mar.1867 aged 62. Their family ROBERT d.10 May 1846 aged 1, MARGARET wife of WILLIAM LEMON d.15 Mar.1889 aged 60. Bottom: 8 lines verse.

	1821		
WILLIAM IRVINE shoemaker in	A	T	
Cairniehillock who d.5 Feb.181-?			
aged 79. J.T. And of their	J	J	
children GEORGE d. 27 Aug	JAMES TAYLOR		
.......ged 47 years	d.23 Apr.1820 aged 15.		

1847. In memory of ALEXANDER IRVINE once tenant in Burnside of Maryculter d.11 Apr.1826 aged 46. JACOBINA MURRAY his wife d.11 July 1846 aged 68. Of their children ALEXANDER d.27 Oct.1846 aged 31.

1873. Erected by JAMES MILNE farmer Netherley. To the memory of the said JAMES MILNE d.21 Dec.1881 aged 71. His wife ANN WYLLIE d.23 Mar.1889 aged 79. ANNIE his only dau. & wife of JOHN DUNCAN late of Reinchall - she d.1 May 1871 aged 19. HELEN MILNE his sister d.25 Oct.1880 aged 77. His son ALEXANDER d.New-York (sic) 17 Feb.1885 aged 44.

1862. Erected by ALEXANDER MILNE blacksmith Netherley in memory of his children: ALEXANDER d.11 Aug.1838 aged 16mths., JOHN d.15 Mar.1850 aged 10, GEORGE d.17 Dec. 1861 aged 13yrs 11mths. Said ALEXANDER MILNE d.17 Sept.1865 aged 61.

1860. Erected by GEORGE LEES & MARGARET CHRISTIE Skatera to the memory of the said GEORGE LEES d.7 Apr.1905 aged 77. MARGARET CHRISTIE his wife d.26 Sept.1861 aged 33./

145 /MARGARET LEES their dau. d.20 Feb.1860 in 4th year. His grandson ROBERT LEES d.20 June
cont. 1892 aged 8mths. His wife HELEN ALLAN d.8 Oct.1927 aged 88.

1868. AH. EH. In memory of ANDREW HOGG tenant in Bents of Muchalls d.28 Oct.1868 aged 70
146 ELIZABETH HOGG his wife d.26 May 1885 aged 84. WILLIAM their son d.28 Apr.1847 aged 15,
ISABELLA their dau. d.13 Feb.1927 in 85th year. ISABELLA their granddau. d.11 June 1889 aged
19.

Erected by WILLIAM TAYLOR farmer Aquhorthies Kingcussie in memory of his wife MAY
147 RITCHIE d.12 Jan.1864 aged 37; Said WILLIAM TAYLOR for 41 years tenant of Aquhorthies d.29
Nov.1908 aged 87. His 2nd wife ISOBEL STRACHAN d.7 May 1911 aged 71. (Heart) In memory
of dear Grandmother d.Windyedge 7 May 1911.

In memory of ALEXANDER TAYLOR d.Aquhorthies 26 Aug.1865 aged 84; ISABELLA MALCOM
148 his wife d.11 Nov.1871 aged 82 & JOHN their son farmer in Aquhorthies, Kingcussie d.6 Nov.1862
aged 35. (Back) 1789. AT. MN. In memory of MARY NAPIER wife of ANDREW TAYLOR d.23
May 1793 aged 57. JOHN son to ANDREW TAYLOR tenant in Aquhorthies d.21 Mar.1789 aged
23.

Erected by GEORGE LEES fisherman Sketraw in memory of his wife ELSPET CRAIG d.21 Nov.
149 1881 aged 62 & of his family MARGARET d.9 Oct.1849 aged 4, ELSPET d.19 Oct.1849 aged 2,
GEORGE d.13 Mar.1856 aged 6. Above GEORGE LEES d.7 June 1904 aged 82.

1850. AL. CC. Erected by CHRISTIAN CHRISTIE in memory of her husband ALEXANDER LEES
150 fisherman Skaterow d.2 Mar.1850 aged 64. Said CHRISTIAN CHRISTIE d.23 Apr.1868 aged 80.
Their dau.MARGARET d.26 Jan.1917 aged 86.

1779. AS. EC. Here lies the Body of ALEXR. STEPHEN late seaman in Sketraw d.17 Mar.1769
151 aged 57; his spouse ELSPET CHRISTE d.10 Sept.1757? aged 36. (Back) In memory of
MARGARET STEPHEN dau. to ye forsaid d.17 Dec.1788 aged 36. (Spellings as on stone)

1849. PL. CC. Erected by PETER LEES Skateraw in memory of his sons ALEXANDER aged 4 &
152 WILLIAM aged 1 who both d.in 1848. His wife CHRISTINA CHRISTIE d.11 May 1883 aged 66.
Above PETER LEES d.11 May 1904 aged 84.

In memory of JOHN LEES d.Stonehaven 7 Dec.1845 aged 74 & JANE SMITH his wife d.7 Nov.
1863 aged 76. Of their family GEORGE d.Quebec 4 July 1838 aged 32, ANDREW late shipmaster
in Stonehaven d.17 Dec.1845 aged 28, JOHN seaman, lost at sea in Oct 1859 aged 46. Their son-in-
law WILLIAM LEES shipmaster d.14 apr.1889 aged 79 & his wife JANE d.4 Feb.1901 aged 95. Of
153 their family JOHN shipmaster lost at sea 31 Dec.1872 aged 40, JANE d.20 May 1904 aged 68,
MARY d.29 Nov.1915 aged 73. (Back) 1806. AL. JS. To the memory of ALEXANDER LEES late
seaman in Cowie d.11 Mar.1804 aged 81; JANNET STEPHEN his spouse d.28 Nov.1805 aged 80.
Of their children JEAN d.14 Nov.1792 aged 20, MARGRET (sic) d.12 Sept.1803 aged 42 &
ALEXR. d.in infancy.

1873. Erected by GEORGE DONALD Westertown of Auchlunies, Maryculter to the memory of
154 MARY HOGG who was his faithful servant for the long period of 40 years. She d.5 Nov.1872 aged
70.

1790. JN. EN. In memory of NOHN NAPIER late seaman in Muchals d.12 Dec.1758 aged 36. (Space) And of JOHN NAPIER their son, smith at Bridge of Muchals d.15 Feb.1788 aged 32.

(Flat) 1772. JT. AB. To the memory of JOHN THOM late tennant in Elrick, he d.7? of Mar.1787 aged 72 also ANN BURNET his spouse d.24 Apr.1779 aged 76. And of their children GEORGE, JOHN, ROBERT, ANN, HELLEN, JAMES, GEORGE? ALEXANDER & WILLIAM .....

(Table) Sacred to the memory of JAMES THOM once tenant in Elrick d.6 Jan.1859 aged 83. His wife MARGARET WILLIAMSON d.4 Jan.1859 aged 82. JAMES THOM of the 4th generation of the name of THOM in Elrick, son of JAMES THOM farmer Elrick d.27 Feb.1841 aged 28.

1812. In memory of JOHN GARROW late tenant in Floors of Feathers d.19 Dec.1803 aged 89; CHRISTIAN FREEMAN his 1st wife d.1 Dec.1781 aged 53. ANNE GARDEN his 2nd wife d.25 Sept.1810 aged 60 & one of their children named ISABEL by the 2nd wife d.27 Nov.1804 aged 18.

Erected by ANNIE CUMMING in memory of her husband JAMES MILNE manager Ivereshie (sic) Kingussie d.Greenheads, Muchalls 20 Aug.1885 aged 42.

(Face very fragile) Erected by HELEN BURNETT in memory of her husband JOHN BARCLAY late taxman at Bridge of Dee Toll d.21 Sept.1851 aged 81.

Erected by GEORGE CHRISTIE fisherman Stonehaven & JANE CHRISTIE his wife in loving memory of their family ELIZABETH d.1 Aug.1882 aged 4mths., JANE d.3 Jan.1884 aged 3yrs 3mths., GEORGINA d.5 May 1885 aged 8mths, ISABELLA d.16 Nov.1890 aged 2, WILLIAM d.6 Apr.1896 aged 15mths. Above JANE CHRISTIE d.30 Sept.1927 aged 73; above GEORGE CHRISTIE d.14 July 1934 aged 79.

Erected by ALEXANDER CHRISTIE & MARGARET LEES his wife in memory of their family: JOHN d.24 July 1873 aged 6mths., JOHN d.26 Nov.1879 aged 5mths., PETER d.3 May 1886 aged 5weeks. Above ALEXR. CHRISTIE d.18 Jan.1910 aged 57; above MARGARET LEES d.3 Dec. 1915 aged 61.

1873. To the memory of JAMES CHRISTIE fisherman Stranathra d.28 Mar.1873 aged 80; MARGARET BRODIE his wife d.28 Apr.1873 aged 75. Their dau.JANE d.16 Mar.1899 aged 59. (Shield) In memory of our dear father & mother WILLIAM & MARGARET CHRISTIE.

1866. In memory of ANNE EDWARDS b.22 Nov.1794 - d.11 June 1866. Erected by the family of the late ARTHUR DUFF ABERCROMBY of Glassaugh & ELIZABETH INNES of Cowie as a mark of esteem & appreciation of her character during the 30 years she resided with them. (Back) To the memory of GEORGE EDWARDS seaman Stonehaven d.4 Sept.1857 aged 82; MARGARET DUNCAN his wife d.16 Aug.1869 aged 97. Their son GEORGE EDWARDS late berthing master Stonehaven d.26 Sept.1891 aged 82 & JESSIE TAYLOR his wife d.3 Jan.1892 aged 76.

Flat stone - nothing visible.

In loving memory of JAMES DUGUID writer d.Stonehaven 28 June 1843 aged 24. His wife ANN EDWARDS d.there 19 Jan.1900 aged 78.

Erected by ELSPET STEPHEN in loving memory of her husband PETER LEES d.8 Oct.1899 aged 31; above ELSPET STEPHEN d.31 Dec.1953 aged 85.

168 Erected by JAMES STEPHEN fisherman Sketraw in memory of his wife MARY MASON d.3 Dec. 1874 aged 63; above JAMES STEPHEN d.7 Apr.1882 aged 74. Their son JAMES STEPHEN fisherman Stonehaven d.14 Oct.1885 aged 48 & his son ALEXANDER d.19 June 1871 aged 3mths. His wife HELEN BRODIE d.6 Nov.1898 aged 54. His son Sapper ADAM STEPHEN 3rd Canadian Engineers killed in action at Poperinghe, Belgium 21 May 1918 aged 36. Bottom: 4 lines verse.

----

169 Erected by ALEXANDER STEPHEN fisherman Stonehaven & his wife ELSPET CAIE in memory of their family: ALEXANDER d.12 Aug.1865 aged 1 mth., a 2nd ALEXANDER d.19 Dec.1867 aged 16mths., JAMES d.4 May 1872 aged 20mths., JOHN d.16 Feb.1874 aged 2 weeks, MARY d.9 Nov.1880 aged 18. Said ALEXANDER STEPHEN d.14 June 1911 aged 68; said ELSPET CAIE d.22 Feb.1934 aged 90. Their grandchild ANDREW STEPHEN d.in infancy. Bottom: 3 lines verse. (Heart in front) AS. EC.

----

170 1847. AS. JM. In memory of - space to ½way down - JOHN STEPHEN son of ALEXANDER STEPHEN seaman in Sketraw d.2 Apr.1847 aged 9 also 2 children d.in infancy.

----

171 Here lies ALLEXR. CADONHEAD who lived in Seatoun of Muchalls dep.11 Dec.1753 aged 63 also ISOBELL CALDER his spouse likewise JAMES, ALLEXR. & REBECKAH CADONHEAD who d.in their infancy.

----

172 In memory of ALEXANDER LEES b.1844 - d.1918, JEAN CHRISTIE his wife b.1845 - d.1918. MARGARET his sister b.1841 - d.1915.

----

173 In memory of JAMIESON NOBLE d.27 Jan.1927 aged 81; his wife FANNY ELIZA CHRISTIE d.10 Apr.1927 aged 74.

----

174 Erected by JAMES O'HARROW in memory of his son DAVID WILLIAM d.23 Oct.1890 aged 3mths., his dau.ROSE d.2 Dec.1911 aged 24. Said JAMES O'HARROW d.11 Sept.1930 aged 80; his wife MARY LINDSAY d.21 Feb.1931 aged 79. His son GEORGE d.6 Aug.1943 aged 48. Bottom: Also in memory of his parents THOMAS O'HARROW d.20 Apr.1864 aged 48, BRIDGET McGOVERN d.4 Apr.1864 aged 43.

----

175 Erected by JOHN & ANN HAMILTON in memory of their children MARGARET d.21 Jan.1857 aged 5, JAMES d.15 May 1863 aged 14, PETER d.31 Jan.1864 aged 21, JANE d.2 July 1865 aged 18. JOHN HAMILTON d.29 Oct.1878 aged 64. ANN MILLIKEN his wife d.7 Apr.1893 aged 74. MARY d.5 Feb.1925 aged 80. (Back) 4 lines verse.

175a (Heart) In loving memory of our mother C.A.W.

----

176 In loving memory of THOMAS HUTCHESON Coast Guard Muchalls d.17 Jan.1890 aged 79; his wife SUSAN BROWNE d.20 July 1891 aged 71. Their sons FREDERICK WILLIAM d.4 Jan.1862 aged 9, ALEXANDER C.WEST d.Sydney, N.S.W. 13 Feb.1870 aged 28. Bottom: 2 lines verse.

----

177 Erected by WILLIAM SOUTER in memory of his son WILLIAM MACKIE d.1 June 1882 aged 4yrs 5mths., his son GEORGE COWIE d.1 Apr.1886 aged 18 mths. His dau.ANN E.M.W.SOUTER d.9 Feb.1904 aged 11. His wife MARGARET MACKIE d.10 Mar.1926 aged 72; above WILLIAM SOUTER d.27 May 1940 aged 89.

----

178 Erected by LIZZIE CAIRD in loving memory of her husband WILLIAM DONALD flesher d.14 July 1900 aged 29. 1 line text.

Erected by MARGARET KNOWLES in loving memory of her husband JAMES BLAIR d.Torry 24 Dec.1906 aged 61; said MARGARET KNOWLES d.Aberdeen 1 July 1916 aged 63. (RHS) In loving memory of my husband JAMES BLAIR d.14 Nov.1945 aged 71; JANE CHRISTIE his wife d.22 July 1954 aged 80. (LHS) Also in memory of their grandchildren JAMES BLAIR b.26 Mar.1899 - d.19 Oct.1900. MAGGIE JANE BLAIR b.29 July 1902 - d.18 Feb.1903. RACHEL BLAIR b.10 Feb. 1904 - d.23 Nov.1904. (Shield on left) In loving memory of JAMES BLAIR b.26 Mar.1899 - d.19 Oct.1900.

1884. Erected by DAVID WILL feuar in Stonehaven in memory of his family: DAVID d.11 Apr. 1879 aged 22, JOHN THOMSON d.30 Aug.1883 aged 19. His wife MARGARET LINTON d.4 May 1888 aged 57; said DAVID WILL d.15 Feb.1901 aged 69. His son WILLIAM d.27 Nov.1908 aged 37. GEORGE THOMSON d.2 Jan.1894 aged 38; ELIZABETH WILL his wife d.22 Feb.1928 aged 69. Their son WILLIAM d.28 July 1907 aged 18. (Back) 1777 AB CD Here lyes the body of ALEXANDER BETTIE late merchant in Stonehaven d.26 June 1777 in 57th year.

Face gone.

1828. GW. IM. In memory of GEORGE WILLIAMSON (space for details but not filled in) ISOBEL MASSON his spouse d.15 June 1827 aged 33 & of their children JEAN d.20 Jan.1826 aged 8, MARGARET d.28 Aug.1826 aged 4, CHRISTIAN d.5 Sept.1826 aged 6, GEORGE d.19 Sept. 1826 aged 17 mths. (Back) In memory of MARGARET CHRISTIE wife of ROBERT WILLIAMSON d.11 Sept.1882 aged 31; said ROBERT WILLIAMSON d.20 June 1908 aged 81.

GA. MC. Here lyes MARGARET CALLDER spouse to GEORGE ADAM seaman in Couie. She d.5 Jully 1753 aged 25 also her child MARGARET ADAM aged 9 mths. (Spellings as on stone)

1805. GG. JC. To the memory of GEORGE GRAY once boat builder in Sketraw d.1 Nov.1790 aged 48; his spouse JANET CHRISTIE d.27 Mar.1811 aged 69. Of their children ALEXR. d.28 Oct. 1797 aged 18, WILLIAM, ANDREW, MARJEORY (sic), GEORGE, JAMES, ALEXR. & ISOBEL who all d.in infancy. (Back) To the memory of WILLIAM MILNE late blacksmith at Windyedge d.11 Apr.1862 aged 95; MARGARET GRAY his wife d.25 Dec.1867 aged 92.

Erected by JANE CHRISTIE in memory of her husband WILLIAM ADAM d.24 Jan.1879 aged 36 & of their family CHRISTINA d.19 Jan.1884 aged 7. Above JANE CHRISTIE d.1 Apr.1926 aged 82. Bottom: 4 lines verse.

Erected by JEAN ADAM in memory of her husband ANDREW ADAM d.3 June 1942 aged 81. Of their family GEORGE d.15 Oct.1908 aged 17, JANE MASSON d.9 Oct.1900 aged 9mths., MARY B.CHRISTIE d.2 Feb.1906 aged 7mths. Above JEAN ADAM d.31 Oct.1948 aged 79.

In loving memory of ALEXANDER ANDREW ADAMS painter Cowie d.12 May 1983 aged 86 and of ALICE GORDON his wife d.13Feb.1992 aged 84. Text.

In memory of WILLIAM HENDERSON mason in Logie d.20 Aug.1805 aged 63 & of ANN BURNET dau.to THOMAS BURNET farmer in Logie & wife of WILLIAM HENDERSON masson (sic) in Logie. She d.11 Sept.1779 aged 36.

1784. AW. JC. In memory of ALEXANDER WATT late seaman in Cowie d.26 Oct.1781 aged 78. (Space) And of their children JOHN, ANDREW, BARBRA, CHRISTIAN & ANN. (Back) In memory of ISABELLA MASSON d.30 Nov.1897 aged 75.

190   Here lies the body of HELLEN DUNCAN spouse to JAMES MILNE blacksmith at Netherley d.9 Apr.1806 aged 78.

(Table) To the memory of DAVID BURNET once Tenant in West town, Logie d.in Stonehaven 29 Jan.1835 aged 81. And SOPHIA DUNCAN spouse of DAVID BURNET tenant in West town of
191   Logie d.31Dec.1807 aged 42. Also GEORGE their son d.10 May 1802 aged 8 and of ANNE THOMSON 2nd wife of DAVID BURNET d.8 Nov.1809 in 41st year. And ANNE their dau.d.24 Sept.1840 aged 48. And CHRISTIAN d.5 Nov.1857 aged 60.

(Flat) GB. JM. (Diptych) (LS) Here lyes ane honest & vertuous man GEORGE BURNET who lived in Sloghead and dep.24 Sept.1740 aged 74.   (RS) Here lyes ane honest and vertuous woman JEAN MEASON spouse to GEORGE BURNET dep.10 Mar.1741 aged 70. (Across the stone) Here lieth
192   ane honest & vertuous man ALEXANDER BURNET dep in Stonehive 10 Aprile 1735 aged 74. Also his son ALERXR. BURNET d.16 Mar.1739 aged 52. AGNES COCKE? his spouse she d.ye 7 Mar. 1741 aged 52. Here also lies GEORGE BURNET son to GEORGE BURNET & CHRISTAN KENNER? who lived in Stonehaven & d.12 May 1769 aged 19.

Sacred to the memory of PETER HENDERSON house carpenter Stonehaven d.7 Mar.1872 aged 58;
193   his wife HELEN WYLLIE d.1 Feb.1871 aged 56. Their children JAMES d.in infancy, PETER d.30 June 1850 aged 4, HELEN d.Montrose 17 Oct.1929 aged 86.

1780. JD. MC. In memory of JOHN DAVIDSON late shoemaker in Montgathead d.26 May 1777 aged 67 also MARGARET CARNEGGIE his spouse d.ye 30 June 1777 aged 63. WILLIAM DAVIDSON Eastside d.22 Aug.1838 aged 82. Renewed by his widow ELIZABETH CHALMERS
194   1847. (Back) In memory of WILLIAM DAVIDSON once subtenant in Easter Acquhollie (space but no details) also MARY SPENCE his wife d.23 Apr.1820 aged 68 & of their children WILLIAM d.27 May 1801 aged 6, MARGARET d.4 June 1801 aged 15, JAMES d.24 June 1805 aged 24, MARY d.23 Nov.1806 aged 22.

----

195   Flat stone - nothing seen.

----

196   AC. MB. In memory of MARGARET BURNET spouse to ALEXANDER COLLISON merchant in Stonehaven - she d.23 Feb.1779 aged 41. Their dau.MARY d.in infancy 19 July 1773.

Erected by JAMES CHRISTIE Sketraw in loving memory of his father ANDREW CHRISTIE d.23
197   Feb.1910 aged 79 & JANE CHRISTIE his mother d.8 Feb.1912 aged 78. His wife JESSIE MacCONACHIE d.14 Sept.1926 aged 38; above JAMES CHRISTIE d.8 Aug.1952 aged 79.

In loving memory of ANDREW MASSON d.19 Nov.1914 aged 65; ISABELLA LEES his wife d.17
198   July 1927 aged 66. Their family ROBERT d.23 Oct.1893 aged 6, GEORGE d.in infancy, JESSIE d.2 Dec.1918 aged 22, ANDREW d.Dunville, Canada 13 Sept.1958 aged 64.

----

199   (Most of the face gone) ....AGNES...dau. d.2 Jan.....(odd bits around, one with ANDREW S... but no way of knowing if they belong to this)

1788. JM. CL. In memory of JOHN MASSON late seaman in Cowie d.7 Sept.1786 aged 61 also
200   CHRISTIAN LEES his spouse d.5 Aug.1787 aged 67. Her son ALEX. MASSON d.3 Sept.1761 aged 9 & BARBARA d.in infancy. Their son ANDREW d.10 May 1790 aged 33.

In loving memory of ROBERT MASSON fisherman Cowie d.15 Jan.1909 aged 82 & of his wife ELISABETH CHRISTIE d.7 Feb.1911 aged 81. Their only son ROBERT was lost at sea 27 Apr. 1889 aged 24; their eldest dau.ELIZABETH d.21 May 1938 aged 75.

ANDREW & CHRISTIAN MASSON. 7 Jan.1834. Here lies interred the partner of my life, a tender mother & a virtuous wife - 8 lines in all. And of her children CHRISTIAN d.in infancy, JOHN d.at sea 7 July 18-- aged 20, JANE d.14 Apr.1834 aged 12/42? (Broken in half & top now face down)

1845. JAMES & WILLIAM MASSON erected this stone in memory of their father ANDREW MASSON d.Bervie 1 Dec.1844 aged 61. Capt. WILLIAM MASSON d.in the North Sea 4 July 1851 aged 31; his dau. ELIZABETH MASSON d.Johnsheaven (sic) 22 July 1852 aged 5yrs. 2mths. MARGARET MAY MASSON his 2nd dau.d.4 Oct.1856 aged 7 & is interred in the Churchyard of Benholm. ELIZABETH wife of ALEXANDER REID shipmaster Montrose d.4 Dec.1857 aged 32. Their dau. MARGARET d.28 Sept.1856 aged 11 mths & lies interred in the Old Churchyard, Montrose.

JC. EC. Here lies the body of JAMES CADDONHEAD late sea-man in Muchall d.1 Dec.1738 aged 46. Their children ALEX aged 10, ISOBEL d.in infancy. ELSPET CALDER his wife d.Dec.1777 aged 74 & JOHN & ROBERT who d.abroad. JAMES d.in June 1767 aged 20, JAMES MASON their great grandchild d.in infancy.

1844. JB. JW. In memory of JAMES BLAIR d.16 Sept.1861 aged 75; his wife JANE WILLIAMSON d.18 Dec.1873 aged 76. Their grandchild JANE LEES d.29 Aug.1877 aged 28. Her child ISABELLA M.DALLAS d.5 Sept.1877 aged 1yr 3mths. JAMES BLAIR their son d.1 Jan.1842 aged 25 & MARGARET d.in infancy. (Heart in front) In memory of our mother CHRISTINA MONCRIEFF aged   52 also our father ROBERT MONCRIEFF aged 83.

Erected by ELIZABETH CHRISTIE in memory of her husband HENRY VALENTINE slater Stonehaven d.1 July 1861 aged 46. Above ELIZABETH CHRISTIE d.11 Aug.1892 aged 74. Their son HENRY d.Edinburgh 29 Sept.1884 aged 36. Bottom: Also in memory of her parents PETER CHRISTIE rope & twine manufacturer Stonehaven d.29 May 1862 aged 88, ELIZABETH MILLAR his wife d.10 Nov.1861 aged 82. Text.

Here resteth in Christ the body of ELSPET WISHART d.in The School House, Stranathara 15 June 1876 aged 82 - for 28 years she taught a school in connexion (sic) with St.Ternan's Church, Muchalls. Bottom: Text.

Erected by JOHN BRODIE fisherman Torry in loving memory of his wife ANNIE CHRISTIE d.11 Mar.1908 aged 38. His grandchild JAMES C.BRODIE d.12 May 1932 aged 3mths. His brother ROBERT BRODIE d.17 May 1953 aged 80. His granddau. HELEN B.LINDSAY wife of JAMES MOIR d.5 May 1958 aged 37. Above JOHN BRODIE d.19 Dec.1962 aged 96.

1857. AB. MC. ALEXANDER BRODIE & MARGARET CRAIG residing in Skaterow. To the memory of ALEXANDER BRODIE d.27 May 1884 aged 78 & MARGARET CRAIG his wife d.8 Sept.1873 aged 70. Their children JEAN d.27 Feb.1837 aged 13mths., MARGARET d.8 Nov.1848 aged 10, ALEXANDER d.23 Sept.1857 aged 26. Also in loving memory of HELEN MAIN wife of JAMES BRODIE Torry d.24 Apr.1914 aged 72. The said JAMES BRODIE d.8 Dec.1926 aged 83; their dau. MARGARET d.29 Apr.1934 aged 63.

---

210   (Cross in front of 209) In loving memory of my mother HELEN MAIN wife of JAMES BRODIE.
Erected by her dau.MAGGIE. Text.

Erected to the memory of JOHN BRODIE b.3 Dec.1833 - d.26 Aug.1908 & MARGARET MASSON
211   his wife b.8 June 1833 - d.20 May 1910. Their son ALEXANDER b.3 Oct.1872 - lost at sea Oct.
1900.

----

212   1742. JF. Here leys JAMES FALCONER boat master Stonhive d.27 Jan.1742 aged 54. (Back) MS.
(Heart in front) In loving memory of JEANIE LOVIE.

Erected by JAMES BRODIE in memory of his father JAMES BRODIE fisherman Cowie d.21 May
213   1883 aged 55 & his mother ANN MASSON d.23 May 1902 aged 69. Above JAMES BRODIE d.26
Sept.1931aged 64; his wife ELSPET WOOD d.13 Jan.1940 aged 72.

Erected in memory of ROBERT TAYLOR Cowie d.18 Apr.1931 aged 54; his wife FRANCES
214   CHRISTIE d.4 Feb.1907 aged 27. Their children JANE ANN d.3 June 1906 aged 10mths., ROBERT
d.30 June 1906 aged 11mths. His 2nd wife ISABELLA K.TAYLOR d.10 Dec.1964 aged 88. Also
their dau. ANNIE d.22 Mar.1992 aged 78.

1860. This stone is erected by JOHN & RUTH PERRIN both natives of Cottagebrooke, North-
hamptonshire (sic) England in memory of their children viz: MARY H. d.Polbare 24 Nov.1836 aged
8, MATILDA R. d. in Dec.1836 aged 16mths., MARGARET BARCLAY ALLARDYCE d.4 June
1860 aged 24. Their granddau. JESSIE MATILDA LEES d.26 Apr.1859 aged 2. Said RUTH
215   PERRIN d.4 May 1874 aged 72; said JOHN PERRIN d.16 Jan.1880 aged 80. Also GEORGE
TAWSE husband of MARTHA PERRIN d.10 Oct.1893 aged 69. (Back) To the memory of MARY
H. PERRIN wife of ROBERT WINTEN d.27 June 1871 aged 31 & of their children MARGARET
d.14 June 1865 aged 1, JOHN T. d.16 Apr.1871 aged 3yrs 8mths., MARY H. d.7 May 1871 aged 22
days. (lower down) ANDREW LEES seaman lost at sea   29 Nov.1864 aged 32.

Erected by JOHN, JAMES & MARY ROSE MILNE in memory of their parents MARY FORBES
216   d.17 Aug.1868 aged 43 & Capt. ANDREW MILNE d.3 Oct.1879 aged 66. Their children JESSIE &
ANDREW d.in infancy, their dau.MARY ROSE wife of WILLIAM COURT BONIFACE d.Sydney,
Australia 12 Oct.1931.

----

217   (Very fragile) In memory of MARY BLAIR spouse of JOHN RITCHIE shipmaster in Stonehaven
d.15 Dec.1810 aged 38.

Erected by ARTHUR CHRISTIE & ELIZABETH WOOD his wife in loving memory of their family
CATHERINE d.10 Jan.1904 aged 13mths., MARY d.10 Apr.1909 aged 16mths., GEORGE, Howe
218   Batt., R.N.D. killed in action in France 13 Aug.1917 aged 23, DONALD d.22 Nov.1918 aged 30,
PETER d.7 July 1933 aged 41. Above ARTHUR CHRISTIE d.16 Dec.1934 aged 71; ELIZABETH
WOOD his wife d.4 Feb.1936 aged 72. Bottom: 2 lines verse. (Now face down)

----

219   In loving memory of my husband WILLIAM H.MARTIN late S.O.H.M.Coast Guard Muchalls d.7
Mar.1903 aged 49.

Erected by ANN WOOD in affectionate remembrance of her husband ALEXANDER CHRISTIE
R.N.R. who while on service d.Larne Hospital, Ireland 16 Feb.1918 aged 50. Their children
220   MAGGIE d.5 Feb.1901 aged 4, JAMES WOOD d.9 Jan.1904 aged 2, JAMES WOOD d.23 Jan.1915
aged 7, MARY ELENOR (sic) d.23 Oct.1923 aged 16, WILLIAM d.27 June 1930 aged 20½. Above/

cont./ANN WOOD d.21Mar.1958 aged 86.

(Table) 1778. JT. Here lyes the Body of the Rev. Mr. JOHN TROUP late Episcopal Minister at Muchalls dep.at Muchalls 17 Aug.1776 aged 75. And REBECCA MOUAT his spouse d.4 June 1791 aged 77. Also 3 of their children ISOBEL, REBECCA & IRVINE.

1837. To the memory of Rev. GEORGE GARDEN who for 41 years was minister of the Episcopal congregation of Stonehaven d.13 Nov.1834 aged 72.

(Flat) In memory of the worthy & Rev. Mr. ROBERT THOMSON Episcopal Minister at Stonehive d.ye 7 of Nov.1737 aged 75. Also the Body of Mrs ANN LINDSAY his spouse. She d.ye 24 May 1729 aged 68.

1779. JF. JC. In memory of JAMES FORREST late blacksmith in Stonehaven d.14 Jan.1779 aged 71. Their children MARGRET (sic) & JEAN d.in infancy. (Back) Capt. GEORGE ADAM d.8 Nov.1895 aged 65; his wife MARGARET FORREST d.27 Dec.1918 aged 85.

(W.G.) A.B.D.FORREST Able Seaman RN J/29457 HMS 'Vivid' 20 Sept.1918 aged 21.

Erected by ANDREW CHRISTIE & HELEN LEES his wife in memory of their family ELSPET d.27 Apr.1885 aged 9mths., MARY d.12 Oct.1887 aged 1yr.3mths., GEORGE d.6 Nov.1893 aged 2yrs. 9mths., JANET d.24 Jan.1896 aged 10mths., JAMES MURRAY d.17 May 1909 aged 3, ANDREW d.25 Oct.1918 aged 25. Above HELEN LEES d.24 Feb.1929 aged 65; above ANDREW CHRISTIE d.19 June 1937 aged 72.

In memory of THOMAS MOIR farmer South Backburn, Ury d.25 Nov.1883 aged 77; ISABELLA BISSET his wife d.16 June 1889 aged 76. Their sons THOMAS d.8 July 1871 aged 23, WILLIAM farmer South Backburn, Ury d.2 Feb.1917 aged 75. (Back) 1828. JM. MC. In memory of (space) and of their children ANDREW MOIR d.in Links of Arduthie 22 Oct.1826 in 23rd year also ROBERT d.in infancy.

(Very fragile) Erected to the memory of ANDREW CHRISTIE d.20 July 1882 aged 73 & MARY McLEOD his wife d.9 Mar.1866 aged 56. Their family WILLIAM aged 51, ANDREW aged 48, THOMAS aged 46 & PETER aged 44 who were all lost at sea 21 Apr.1880. MARGARET LEIPER wife of WILLIAM CHRISTIE d.18 Feb.1921 aged 92.

(Initials only) M.C.

In loving memory of my husband JAMES BLAIR d.31 Jan.1944 aged 64.

Erected by ANN LEIPER in loving memory of her husband ROBERT LEES d.23 Feb.1923 aged 65; above ANN LEIPER d.3 Nov.1929 aged 76. Their son ROBERT d.16 Nov.1939 aged 59, husband of JANE ADAM.

Erected by MARY MASSON in memory of her husband ROBERT LEES fisherman d.18 Apr.1898 aged 70. Their family JOHN & ANDREW d.in infancy, WILLIAM d.12 Dec.1910 aged 39. Said MARY MASSON d.15 Jan.1915 aged 85. 1 line text.

Erected by JEAN M.CRIGGIE in loving memory of her husband CHARLES LEES d.23 Jan.1929 aged 65. Their family Cpl.CHARLES LEES 7th Gordon Hrs. fell in action at Arras 23 Apr.1917/

233   /aged 24. Pte. RITCHIE LEES 4th Gordon Hrs. killed in France 25 May 1916 aged 19, ROBERT d.9
cont. Mar.1906 aged 15, WILLIAM d.16 Mar.1909 aged 4, JANE d.in infancy. Above JEAN M.CRIGGIE
       d.15 Apr.1944 aged 75.

----

234   In loving memory of my husband WILLIAM LEES d.12 Dec.1910 aged 39. His wife MARGARET
      JANE CLARK d.2 Dec.1952 aged 83.

      Erected by ANDREW LEES whitefisher Stonehaven in memory of his children MARGARET d.17
      Feb.1864 aged 14, JANE DICKSON d.22 Jan.1864 aged 2 yrs.9 mths. MARGARET LEES his wife
      d.17 Oct.1880 aged 56; above ANDREW LEES d.14 Mar.1899 aged 80. Bottom: And of his father
      ANDREW LEES d.28 Oct.1866 aged 80; his mother MARGARET TAYLOR d.9 Mar.1839 aged 63.
235   (Back) ALEXANDER LEES b.14 June 1876 - d.18 Aug.1878; FREDRICK LEES b.2 Apr.1878 -
      d.29 June 1887 & their father ANDREW LEES tailor d.3 July 1898 aged 45. JANE BARRACK
      LEIPER his wife d.16 May 1911 aged 58. In memory also of ARTHUR WELLESLEY KINNEAR
      LEES grandson of said ANDREW LEES d.21 Feb.1968 aged 56 & MARGARET ADA his wife d.15
      Sept.1969 aged 64.

----

236   (Square) In loving memory of our dear aunt SUSAN LEES.

      Erected to the memory of JOHN LEES fisherman Cowie d.30 Apr.1923 aged 75; his wife HELEN
237   BLAIR d.27 Dec.1941 aged 83. Of their family JOHN accidentally drowned in USA 9 July 1908
      aged 23, ROBERT R.N.R. killed on active service 12 July 1917 aged 19, ISABELLA d.12 Nov.1955
      aged 68, ALEXANDER & ANDREW.

      JC. IO. Erected by JOHN CHRISTIE boat builder Skeatrow in memory of his spouse ISABEL OGG
      d.27 Feb.1840 aged 25. JOHN his son d.4 Mar.1855 aged 4 mths., ALEXANDER d.6 May 1881
      aged 25, JAMIMA (sic) d.16 Nov.1893 aged 25. Said JOHN CHRISTIE d.in 1896, Dec.11 aged 83.
238   ANN STRACHAN his 2nd wife d.8 Aug.1907 aged 79. His grandson FREDRICK JOHN CHRISTIE
      d.Glasgow 13 July 1912 aged 12. (Back) Also his dau.-in-law MARY STEWART d.25 Jan.1940
      aged 71 & ANDREW CHRISTIE her husband d.20 Oct.1953 aged 89. (Heart) Our dear sister
      JEMIMA.

      GC. MO. In memory of GEORGE CHRISTIE boat-builder Sketraw d.12 May 1849 aged 31; MARY
239   OGG his wife d.23 Aug.1899 aged 82. Of their children MARY d.28 Jan.1848 aged 4, GEORGE
      clerk, Joint Station, Aberdeen d.14 July 1879 aged 30. (Back) 1849.

----

240   1779. In memory of GEORGE BURNET late maltster in Stonehaven dep.3 Mar..... aged 80.

----

241   (Cross) MARY TOMPER d.17 Dec.1859 aged 4mths.

      1874. Erected by ALEXANDER BREBNER cooper Stonehaven in memory of his children:
242   ALEXANDER d.10 July 1856 aged 11, WILLIAM STRACHAN school master d.21 Oct.1872 aged
      25. HELEN STRACHAN his wife d.31 Aug.1883 aged 72; above ALEXANDER BREBNER d.21
      Mar.1893 aged 76. His dau. JANE d.6 July 1926 aged 85. 5 lines text.

      Erected by JANET MASSON Skaterow in memory of her husband ALEXANDER CHRISTIE d.5
      Apr.1872 aged 46; said JANET MASSON d.25 July 1915 aged 84. Of their family ALEXANDER
243   d.14 July 1864 aged 10mths., JANET d.10 Nov.1864 aged 4, ANDREW d.12 Jan.1870 aged
      12mths., JOHN d.13 Apr.1872 aged 16mths. Also in loving memory of ROBERT CHRISTIE son of
      WILLIAM CHRISTIE & husband of ELSIE M.CRAIG d.Stonehaven 30 Dec.1918 aged 37./

/MARGARET LEES wife of above WILLIAM CHRISTIE d.4 Aug.1942 aged 81; said WILLIAM
CHRISTIE d.4 Dec.1944 aged 89. 4 lines verse.

AS. CB. In memory of ALEXANDER STRACHAN shoemaker in Stonehaven d.15 Dec.1778 aged
83? .....BURNETT his spouse d.-- Feb.1807 aged 66. Also FRANCIS STRACHAN.....late baker
in Stonehaven .... rest of face gone.

Erected by ANDREW LEES fisherman in memory of his wife HELEN MASSON d.5 June 1912
aged 49. His dau. MARGARET d.16 June 1929 aged 5½. Above ANDREW LEES d.30 July 1930
aged 64; his 2nd wife MARGARET SARAH DONALD d.8 Sept.1948 aged 57. (Vase in front)
ANDREW & MARGARET LEES.

1855. Erected by ANDREW LEES to the memory of his wife JEAN MASSON d.Skaterow 1
Apr.1855 aged 29. PETER his son d.25 Apr.1878 aged 10mths. Above ANDREW LEES d.11 Jan.
1886 aged 58; his 2nd wife JANE CHRISTIE d.15 Apr.1925 aged 86. Bottom: 4 lines verse.

(Bottom RHS off) AB. CB. Here lies ALEX BURNET who lived in Couie dep.26 May 1747 aged
69 also CHRISTIEAN (sic) BURNET his spouse d.30 Mar.17-- aged 80. Also THOMAS BURNET
d.-- Nov.1735....... Bottom: 17 AB I- ....

Erected by ALEXANDER CARNEGIE millwright Grandholm in memory of his spouse ELSPET
CHRISTIE d.14 Apr.1847 aged 38. Of their children ANDREW aged 5mths & ELSPET aged
13mths. Said ALEXANDER CARNEGIE late of Port Elphinstone d.Aberdeen 19 Jan.1885 aged 76.

Erected by PETER TESTER salmon fisher Muchalls in memory of his wife ANN MAIN d.27 Jan.
1872 aged 41. His daus. ELIZABETH d.6 Aug.1861 aged 1, JANE d.4 Sept.1925 aged 67. Bottom:
And of his parents JAMES TESTER d.22 Nov.1873 aged 77.

Sacred to the memory of ANN REITH spouse to ANDREW CHRISTIE boat builder Sketrow d.27
July 1807 aged 50. Of their children ISABEL & WILLIAM d.in infancy. This stone is erected by
their son ANDREW carpenter in Aberdeen.

Erected by ALEXANDER LEES whitefisher Sketraw in memory of his wife HELEN CHRISTIE
d.23 Mar.1864 aged 33 & of his dau. ANN d.5 Sept.1873 aged 5. His 2nd wife ISABELLA BRODIE
d.22 Oct.1912 aged 71. Above ALEXANDER LEES d.23 Sept.1920 aged 87. ALEXANDER
CHRISTIE husband of ISABELLA LEES d.13 June 1941 aged 70; above ISABELLA LEES d.27
Nov.1941 aged 75.

AC. IT. Here lyes the body of ALEXANDER CHRISTIE late seaman in Sketraw d.24 Mar.1761
aged 61; his wife ISOBEL TAYLOR d.1 May 1784 aged 88. AC. And of his nephew ANDREW
CHRISTIE d.3 June 1795 aged 19.

(Table) Erected by MARGARET CADENHEAD as a tribute of affection & gratitude to the memory
of her cousin ALEXANDER FALCONER who having served at sea for 40 years, a great part of that
time Commander in the Merchant & Transport Services from the Port of London, retired to Stonehaven, his native place where after long living respected he d.regretted 26 July 1837 in 83rd year.
R.I.P.

JF. JF. In memory of the after named JAMES FALCONER d.9 Sept.1804 aged 80. JEAN
FALCONER spouse to JAMES FALCONER seaman in Stonehaven d.1 Mar.1792 aged 71. Of their/

254 /children KATHERINE MARGARET & MARGARET JEAN & GEORGE. JAMES FALCONER
cont. d.6 July 1831 aged 80.

1855. Erected by MARGRET (sic) LEES in memory of her husband ALEXANDER LEES ship
master d.Konigsberg 10 Sept.1852 aged 53. Of their children ROBERT d.Glasgow 1 Sept.1854 aged
15, JOHN ship master d.Stonehaven 3 Sept.1854 aged 27, JAMES ship master d.Ibrial 22 Sept.1856
255 aged 31, ROBERT SIMPSON drowned off the Scilly Islands 24 Jan.1862 aged 19, ALEXANDER
LEES ship master drowned in the North Sea 30 Oct.1863 aged 34, MARGARET WATT d.Stone-
haven 29 Apr.1866 aged 64, CHARLES LEES ship master d.Stonehaven 22 May 1866 aged 34,
MARGARET LEES d.Juniper Green 30 Mar.1907 aged 73.

In loving memory of JAMES LEES shipmaster d.14 Jan.1881 aged 80 & his wife JANE STEPHEN
256 d.4 Dec.1891 aged 88. Their daus. ISABELLA d.20 Oct.1900 aged 62, CHRISTINA d.11 Sept.1901
aged 72.

JAMES CHRISTIE Skaterow to the memory of JAMES his son d.20 July 1831 aged 1,
257 ALEXANDER d.6 Aug.1842 aged 5. MARGARET MASSON his wife d.5 May 1854 aged 57; above
JAMES CHRISTIE d.2 Aug.1870 aged 80.

(Face fragile) Erected by WILLIAM CHRISTIE & JANE LEIPER his wife in loving memory of their
family - JOHN d.21 Mar.1859 aged 3yrs.3mths., PETER d.27 Jan.1862 aged 6mths., ANN d.26 July
258 1868 aged 5yrs 5mths., PETER d.14 May 1870 aged 3yrs.3mths., JANE d.24 July 1889 aged 35.
Above JANE LEIPER d.12 Oct.1900 aged 79; above WILLIAM CHRISTIE d.10 Nov.1900 aged 76.
(Square leaning on the back) In loving memory of our dear MAGGIE d.19 Nov.1911 aged 28.

Erected by JAMES CHRISTIE in loving memory of his wife ANN CHRISTIE d.Aberdeen 5 Feb.
259 1905 aged 63. Said JAMES CHRISTIE d.there 25 June 1909 aged 60. Of their family ANN d.27
Feb.1878 aged 3, HELEN d.27 Mar.1880 aged 1.

(2 stones) In loving memory of my husband ANDREW CHRISTIE d.21 Oct.1939 aged 70 & his
wife MARGARET LEES d.6 Nov.1959 aged 88. (Stone 2) RC. IM. In memory of ISOBEL
260 MIDDELTOWN (sic) spouse to ROBERT CORMACK late seaman in Cowie d.7 June 1762 aged
34. Their dau. JANT. CORMACK late spouse to ROBERT LAW seaman in Cowie d.11 Feb.1786
aged 30.

Erected by THOMAS CHRISTIE Skaterow in memory of his wife JANET MASSON d.20 Mar.1873
261 aged 37; said THOMAS CHRISTIE drowned at sea 21 Apr.1880 aged 46. (Heart in front) WL. In
loving memory of dear mother d.Oct.1872.

---

262 1791. AB. EC. In memory (space) of ELSPIT CAIRD the wife of ANDREW BURNET farmer in
Colts d.20 May 1794 aged 70 & of their dau. HELEN BURNET d.8 Dec.1790 aged 31.

1795. JH. HB. In memory of JOHN HENDERSON late tenant in Nibbetstone of Durris b.12 Jan.
1728 - d.21 May 1809 & HELEN BURNETT his wife b.24 Jan.1732 - d.31 Dec.1813. Also of JOHN
HENDERSON their son dep.Glithnow 8 Feb.1793 in 29th year; GEORGE d.in infancy. (Back) The
263 family of JOHN HENDERSON & HELEN BURNETT: ANN HENDERSON b.11 May 1760 -
d.Mains of Durris 10 Dec.1817; HELEN HENDERSON b.30 May 1762 - d.Brackmuirhill 19 Aug.
1838; JOHN HENDERSON late tailor at Glithnow b.23 Apr.1764 - d.8 Feb.1793; DAVID late
blacksmith at Arnhall b.3 Aug.1766 - d.24 Feb.1844 - buried at Fettercairn. ALEXANDER late
mason Johnshaven b.4 Sept.1768 - d.27 Nov.1843, buried at Benholm; GEORGE & another son/

/who both d.in infancy. ANDREW late tenant in Glithnow b.19 Aug.1772 - d.23 July 1839. Repaired in 1846 by ROBERT HENDERSON mason at Ury b.3 Dec.1775 - d.24 Nov.1847.

(Flat) Here lyes the Body of ANNA JOHNSTON spouse to JOHN SMART Farmer in Crosleay d.28? Dec.1783 aged 60. Also of the said JOHN SMART d.26 May 1797 aged 66. HELEN DUNN widow of PETER MATHIESON shipmaster d.Cookney Cottage 13 Mar.1892 aged 88. And of LUCIE SMART their dau. d.5 Feb.1799 aged 3. Bottom: Also JAMES SMART for 32 years schoolmaster at Cookney, grandson of above JOHN SMART d.10 May 1911 aged 90 & of his spouse ISABELLA MATHIESON d.9 Sept.1912 aged 87.

Erected by A.GORDON SMART in affectionate remembrance of ANNIE MORTON NAIRN a loving wife & mother d.14 May 1922 aged 62; above A.GORDON SMART d.5 Jan.1946 aged 84.

Erected by MARGARET LEES and family in loving memory of her husband JAMES LEES d.30 Apr.1917 aged 48. Above MARGARET LEES d.26 Sept.1947 aged 78. Their dau. JANE CHRISTIE d.3 Feb.1954 aged 63. (Shield in front) In loving memory of 'wee' MARGARET J.MUNRO.

GEORGIUS IRONSIDE Eccl.Scot.Sacerdos in Xto obdormivit iiij Non.Oct.MDCCCLXI (1861) DET ILLI DOMINUS INVENIRE MISERICORDIAM A DOMINO IN ILLA DIE.

Beneath in hope etc. rest the remains of Rev. JAMES SMITH for 27 years pastor of the Episcopal congregation of Muchals dep.16 Mar.1854 aged 52. This stone has been erected by the members of his congregation as testimony of gratitude for the care he bestowed on their wants both spiritual and temporal. Here also lie the remains of ISABELLA dau.of above aged 5. 3 lines text. Also OLIVIA RUSSELL his wife d.5 Dec.1885 aged 75. CHARLOTTE RAMSDEN SMITH dau. d.14 June 1923.

In memory of GEORGE MELLES late tenant at Muchals d.18 Oct.1816 aged 66; his wife MARGARET REA d.17 July 1849 aged 96. Their daus.MARY d.31 Oct.1834 aged 66, ANN d.14 Apr.1844 aged 64, MARGARET d.21 Nov.1856 aged 68.

In loving memory of JOHN KNOWLES d.8 Feb.1901 aged 53. His sons ROBERT d.26 Mar.1883 aged 1, WILLIAM d.7 Dec.1898 aged 14. His son-in-law EDWARD JOHN NEWDICK A.B., R.N. torpedoed in the Dardanelles 25 May 1915 aged 26. His grandson EDWARD JOHN DUFFIELD d.in infancy. CHRISTINA CHRISTIE wife of above JOHN KNOWLES d.2 Nov.1933 aged 82. ANDREW KNOWLES their son d.Doncaster 4 June 1938 aged 57. (Heart in front) In loving memory of our dear children. A.C.

Erected by GEORGE ARTHUR in loving memory of his dau. HELEN JANE d.30 Aug.1904 aged 14; said GEORGE ARTHUR d.28 Feb.1921 aged 64. His son WILLIAM d.8 June 1937 aged 48; also JANE WALKER his wife d.27 July 1953 aged 90. His daus. MARY ISABELLA d.29 Apr.1975 aged 73, MARGARET INGRAM d.13 Apr.1977 aged 84. Bottom: Also JANE WALKER d.15 Feb. 1923 aged 80.

In memory of ANNIE beloved dau. of JOHN MOIR gamekeeper Cowie d.26 Dec.1904 aged 21. His wife ANN LYON DUNN d.21 Nov.1928 aged 77; above JOHN MOIR d.5 May 1929 aged 79.

Erected by SAMUEL LYON & CHRISTINA DEANS his wife in memory of their son JOHN d.Banbury, W.A. 19 Dec.1913 aged 38. Above SAMUEL LYON d.8 July 1919 aged 64; above CHRISTINA DEANS d.1 Feb.1928 aged 73.

Erected by their family in memory of their parents CHARLES DONALD tenant in Wyndyedge d.14 Feb.1836 aged 91; CHRISTIAN PATERSON his wife d.10 May 1836 aged 57. JAMES their son d.in infancy. Their son ANDREW sometime farmer at Wyndyedge d.Newtonhill 12 Apr.1888 aged 86. JOHN WILSON platelayer L.M.S. Ry. d.Glithno Cottage, Ury 12 May 1933 aged 80; his wife
274 ISABELLA DEANS d.6 May 1938 aged 85 & JEAN WOOD their grandchild d.10 Sept.1860 aged 14. (Back) In memory of JAMES WOOD tenant in Auchinhar, Elsick d.18 Oct.1861 aged 46; JEAN DONALD his wife d.8 Feb.1864 aged 48. Of their children JAMES d.2 Feb.1862 aged 10, CHRISTINA P. d.13 June 1862 aged 3, JOHN d.12 Mar.1863 aged 8, ISABELLA D. d.15 Apr.1864 aged 21, ANDREW D. d.16 Apr.1868 aged 19. ISABELLA DONALD wife of GEORGE DEANS d.4 Nov.1866 aged 46.

1839. In memory of WILLIAM DUNCAN late gardener at Barras d.Brackmuirhill 23 Mar.1839
275 aged 81 & HELEN HENDERSON his wife d.19 Aug.1838 aged 78. ANDREW his brother, for many years servant to LEWIS INNES Esq. of Bennycraig d.Brackmuirhill 4 July 1833 aged 85. Erected by WILLIAM FRASER shoemaker Upper Banchory, their nephew.

In loving memory of ALEXANDER DONALDSON slater d.25 July 1888 aged 54 & MARJORY
276 MITCHELL his wife d.29 Mar.1891 aged 56. Of their family DAVID d.in infancy 1876, ANN d.1 Feb.1890 aged 26, MARGARET d.5 July 1936 aged 69. MARY wife of JOHN MUIR d.Edinburgh 13 Nov.1942.

1862. In memory of ALEXANDER WALKER d.Cairngrassie 8 Mar.1851 aged 84; ELIZABETH
277 BROWN his wife d.29 Jan.1862 aged 82. Of their children GEORGE d.2 May 1824 aged 6, ANN d.23 May 1824 aged 3, DAVID d.11 Apr.1904 aged 78.

(Top gone) (Erected by ELSPET CHRISTIE in memory of her husband ANDREW) LAW d.27 Apr.1901 aged 53?. Of their children HELEN d.in infancy, ANDREW d.22 Nov.1879 aged 5,
278 ANDREW d.15 Sept.1888 aged 1yr.5mths., HELEN d.7 June 1894 aged 12. Above ELSPET CHRISTIE d.10 July 1922 aged 78. Their son-in-law DAVID COWIE MAIN Chief Stoker R.N. d.2 Aug.1941 aged 63 & MARY ANN GRACE LAW his wife d.22 Sept.1952 aged 74. 2 lines verse.

Erected by JOHN CHRISTIE & ISABELLA MASSON his wife in loving memory of their family: WILLIAM d.26 Dec.1870 aged 14mths., ALEXANDER d.in infancy 1873, ISABELLA d.9 Jan.1884
279 aged 16yrs 9mths. Above ISABELLA MASSON d.3 Apr.1908 aged 73; above JOHN CHRISTIE d.8 July 1909 aged 76. Also in memory of the children of WILLIAM CHRISTIE: JESSIE d.5 Sept.1909 aged 3mths., KATIE d.16 Oct.1915 aged 8, MARY d.17 Dec.1918 aged 6, MARGARET d.4 Apr. 1927 aged 6yrs 3mths. 1 line text.

(Cross - leaning against the back of 281 & 282) Erected by ANN CHRISTIE in loving memory of
280 her husband JAMES CHRISTIE d.Sketraw 11 Dec.1919 aged 85; above ANN CHRISTIE d.15 Sept. 1930 aged 94. 1 line text.

Erected by WILLIAM CHRISTIE Sketraw in loving memory of his wife MARGARET CHRISTIE
281 d.24 Dec.1894 aged 67 & of their children WILLIAM d.18 Sept.1859 aged 1, SUSAN d.10 June 1865 aged 2, JANE d.4 Nov.1867 aged 1, JOHN d.7 Sept.1869 aged 1, JAMES d.10 Oct.1884 aged 28, SUSAN d.5 Jan.1895 aged 23. Said WILLIAM CHRISTIE d.6 June 1904 aged 74.

Erected by JANE MASSON in memory of her husband JOHN CHRISTIE fisherman Skaterow d.23
282 Feb.1883 aged 80; said JANE MASSON d.22 Dec.1889 aged 82. Their son JOHN d.8 June 1909 aged 77; his wife MARGARET CHRISTIE d.21 May 1923 aged 88. His son JOHN d.4 May 1865/

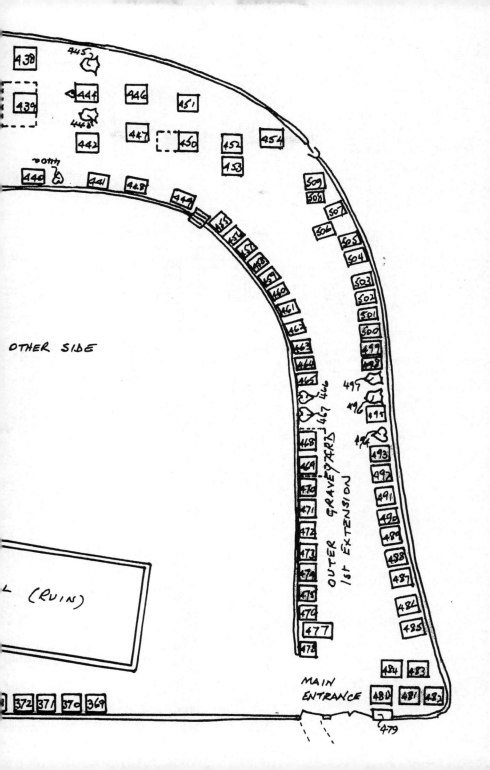

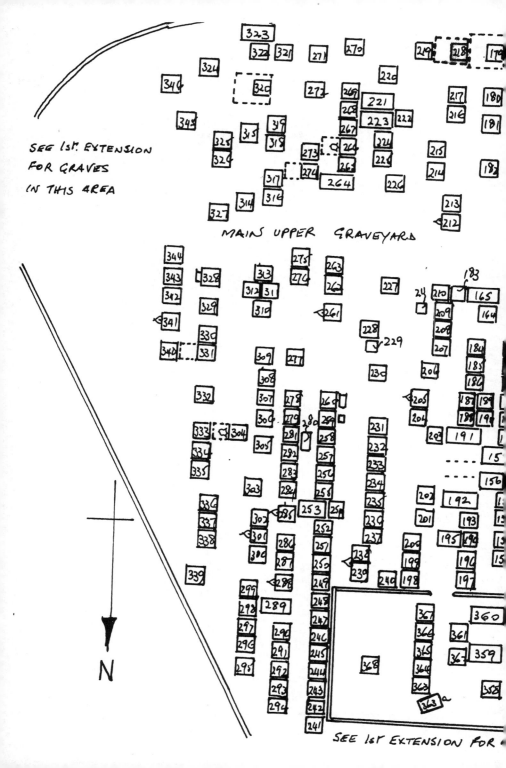

SEE 1st. EXTENSION
FOR GRAVES
IN THIS AREA

MAINS UPPER GRAVEYARD

N

SEE 1st EXTENSION FOR

COWIE
ST MARY OF THE STORMS

CHAPEL

LOWER GRAVEYARD — SEE 1ST EXTENSION

MAIN ENTRANCE

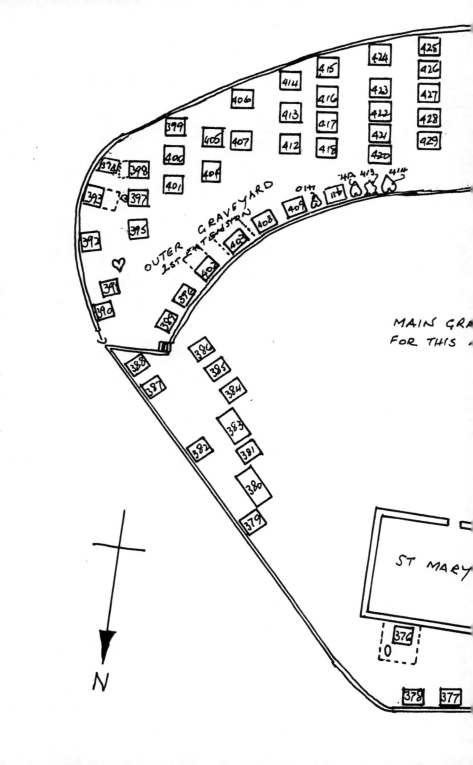

OUTER GRAVEYARD
1ST EXTENSION

MAIN GRA
FOR THIS

ST MARY

N

32 /aged 14mths., his daus. ELIZABETH d.9 Mar.1919 aged 45, HELEN d.7 Oct.1953 aged 82,
nt. ISABELLA d.20 Dec.1960 aged 93.

1860. Erected by ROBERT CHRISTIE & CHRISTIAN MASSON Skateraw to the memory of said
ROBERT CHRISTIE d.1 Feb.1888 aged 62; CHRISTIAN MASSON his wife d.18 Aug.1913 aged
33 82. WILLIAM their son d.31 Mar.1859 in 4th year, JOHN d.in infancy & ANDREW d.20 Feb.1917
aged 59. ROBERT d.14 July 1926 aged 73, JANE d.24 May 1929 aged 57, WILLIAM d.13 Jan.1937
aged 73.

In loving memory of WILLIAM LEES fisherman d.22 Apr.1919 aged 73 & JEAN CHRISTIE his
34 wife d.3 Mar.1924 aged 72. HUGH McLEAN d.23 Jan.1951 aged 63. Bottom: Erected by their son
ALEXANDER.

Erected to the memory of JOHN CHRISTIE Cowie d.21 Feb.1852 aged 55 & ELIZABETH
MASSON his wife d.24 May 1862 aged 66. Of their family PETER d.6 Oct.1868 aged 33, ROBERT
35 d.21 Nov.1884 aged 57, JANE, JOHN & ALEXANDER all d.in infancy. JANE WILLIAMSON wife
of above PETER CHRISTIE d.30 Jan.1911 aged 71. JANE MASSON wife of ROBERT CHRISTIE
d.18 Apr.1931 aged 63. Above ROBERT CHRISTIE d.13 Oct.1949 aged 82 & his dau. EDITH
MARY d.13 Aug.1973 aged 71. (Heart in front) In memory of our dear mother M.M.

(Flaking at bottom) 1826. In memory of JAMES MASSON sea-man in Cowie d.2 Feb.1825 aged
36 61; ISABEL CHRISTIE his wife d.19 Jan.1860 aged 95. Of their children SUSANNA d.1 May 1800
in 7th year, ALEXANDER d.15 May 1800 in 5th year, JAMES d.in infancy.

Erected by JAMES CHRISTIE fisherman Skatrow (sic) in memory of his wife MARY MASSON d.6
Jan.1837 aged 72. Of their children ALEXR. d.Nov.1799 aged 4, ROBERT & ISOBEL d.in infancy,
ANDREW d.Mar.1815 aged 10. Said JAMES CHRISTIE d.17 Mar.1838 aged 84. JAMES
37 CHRISTIE d.Skatrow 24 Dec.1861 aged 66; MARY MASSON his wife d.20 Jan.1878 aged 79. Of
their children WILLIAM d.1837 aged 4, JOHN & PETER d.in infancy. WILLIAM CHRISTIE d.21
Mar.1868 aged 70; ISABELLA CRAIG his wife d.3 May 1876 aged 80. (Back) Sacred to the
memory of JAMES CHRISTIE fisherman Stonehaven d.7 Dec.1884 aged 62; his wife ISABELLA
CHRISTIE d.4 Nov.1888 aged 67. Of their family MARY d.1850 aged 6, WILLIAM d.1867 aged
11, MARY d.14 Jan.1885 aged 32, DAVID d.at sea 24 Jan.1885 aged 21. Bottom: 4 lines text.

1792. JD. KH. To the memory of JOHN DAVIDSON late farmer in Balnagask d.9 Apr.1759 aged
8 63 - a loving husband, a dutifull parent & a support to the poor & needy. KATHARINE HOGG his
spouse d.28 June 1791 aged 88. A virtuous wife & examplary for piety. Of their children ISOBEL
aged 15 & JOHN d.2 July 1784 aged 60. (Spellings as on stone) (Heart in front) HELLEN.

----

9 (Flat stone - not much legible) 1752. JD. MO. Here lyes JAMES DUNCAN late of M...........

RM. 1833. JM. ROBERT MASSON Skaterow. To the memory of ROBERT MASSON d.4 Nov.
1874 aged 80 & JEAN MASSON his wife d.2 Feb.1833 aged 34. His 2nd wife ISABELLA
0 MASSON d.20 Mar.1893 aged 83. MARGARET their dau. d.22 Jan.1858 aged 18. ISABELLA d.24
Feb.1865 aged 23. (Back) Here rests in Christ the body of ROBERT MASSON fisherman Skaterow
d.12 Oct.1876 aged 38; his wife ISABELLA CHRISTIE d.29 Mar.1896 aged 58. Their son
ALEXANDER d.14 Oct.1890 aged 24; their dau. HELEN d.19 May 1895 aged 21. Bottom: 4 lines
verse.

----

291 1849. JAMES & CHRISTIAN MASSON Skateraw. To the memory of JAMES MASSON d.24 May 1857 aged 43; CHRISTIAN MASSON his wife d.13 Jan.1874 aged 58. Of their children MARGARET d.10 Oct.1841 aged 8mths., JEAN d.20 Oct.1848 aged 3, ELSPETH d.7 May 1917 aged 78, CHRISTIAN d.14 Sept.1922 aged 80, widow of THOMAS CHRISTIE fisherman. JAMES son of above JAMES MASSON d.10 Jan.1931 aged 87.

----

292 In memory of BARBARIE BURNET who lived in Stonehaven. She d.15 Jan.1782 aged 61. (Back) CB.

----

293 1878. Erected by ANDREW MASSON & HELEN CHRISTIE in remembrance of their children ISABELLA d.21 Apr.1872 aged 6, MARGARET also d.21 Apr.1872 aged 2. Above ANDREW MASSON d.12 June 1899 aged 61; above HELEN CHRISTIE d.20 Dec.1922 aged 81. Base: 4 lines verse. (White cross in front - broken) In loving memory of our dear father & mother.

----

294 Erected by WILLIAM LEES in loving memory of his wife HELEN MASSON d.5 Dec.1938 aged 64; above WILLIAM LEES d.20 Oct.1956 aged 83.

----

295 Erected by JANNET MASSON in loving memory of her husband JOHN MASSON d.Torry 13 May 1893 aged 28. Above JANET (sic) MASSON d.20 July 1939 aged 75. Their son JOHN d.at sea 8 Nov.1916 aged 32, fisherman, Torry.

----

296 Erected by GEORGE MASSON Sketraw in memory of his wife MARY CHRISTIE d.17 Mar.1899 aged 67; said GEORGE MASSON d.8 Nov.1910 aged 77. Their dau. MARGARET d.22 Feb.1900 aged 30; their son GEORGE d.5 Aug.1928 aged 60.

----

297 In memory of WILLIAM MASSON d.4 May 1873 aged 35 & of his children WILLIAM d.30 Dec. 1865 aged 1yr 2mths., WILLIAM d.26 Dec.1867 aged 1yr 5mths. His wife ELSPET STEPHEN d.12 June 1926 aged 85. MARGARET MAIN wife of JAMES MASSON d.27 Apr.1881 aged 37 & their dau. ELIZABETH d.in infancy. Bottom: 4 lines verse. (Back) 1830. WM. EL. In memory of WILLIAM MASSON seaman Skateraw d.1 Jan.1849 aged 74 & ELSPET LEES his spouse d.11 Apr. 1830 in 55th year. Of their children ALEXANDER d.in infancy. Here lies the body of WILLIAM MASSON d.24 Oct.1846 aged 43; his son (not named) d.1 Jan.1837 in infancy.

----

298 1805. JM. IN. To the memory of JAMES MASON late seaman in Sketraw d.18 Apr.1802 aged 82 & ISOBEL NAPIER his spouse d.20 Dec.1765 aged 40. Of their children ALEXANDER d.Egypt 30 June 1802 aged 33 & ANDREW d.26 Nov.1761 aged 5. JOHN MASSON (sic) seaman in Sketraw d.29 Sept.1836 aged 80 & CHRISTIAN BRODIE his wife d.15 Mar.1834 aged 67. (Back) JM. JM. In memory of JAMES MASSON d.Skateraw 26 May 1881 aged 85; JANE MASSON his wife d.12 July 1879 in 78th year. Of their family ISOBEL d.26 July 1841 aged 6 & ANN d.26 Nov.1848 aged 11. JAMES MASSON d.4 Feb.1921 aged 75; MARGARET MASSON his wife d.18 Jan.1916 aged 73. ISABELLA CHRISTIE wife of GEORGE MASSON d.25 Aug.1905 aged 31.

----

299 1791. AM. MB. In memory of ALEXANDER MASON late seaman in Sketraw d.9 Oct.1788 aged 54 & of their childern (sic) JOHN, ALEXANDER & ELSPIT. (Space left unfilled for wife) (Back) In memory of JAMES MASSON (sic) seaman in Sketraw d.4 Nov.1839 aged 80; JANET ADAM his wife d.16 Apr.1848 aged 81 & 3 of their children who d.in infancy.

----

300 In memory of WILLIAM MASSON d.24 Aug.1843 aged 44; his wife ISABELLA CRAIG d.29 Nov. 1884 aged 84. ISABELLA CHRISTIE wife of WILLIAM MASSON d.22 Dec.1905 aged 81; above WILLIAM MASSON d.2 Mar.1921 aged 92. (Back) JM. IC. Erected by JOHN MASSON Sketraw/

00 /in memory of his spouse ISABEL CHRISTIE d.5 Apr.1829 aged 66 & their dau. ELSPITH d.in
ont. infancy.

In memory of JOHN MORGAN blacksmith d.4 July 1872 aged 46; his wife ISABELLA ADAM d.30
May 1899 aged 65. Of their family ANDREW d.9 Mar.1867 aged 6mths., ISABELLA d.7 Nov.1869
01 aged 19mths., ALEXANDER d.13 July 1894 aged 23, JOHN d.1 Dec.1928 aged 69, AGNES d.19
Sept.1934 aged 77, GEORGE d.17 Aug.1935 aged 71, HELEN d.1 June 1942 aged 84. (Shield in
front) In memory of JOHN MORGAN blacksmith d.July 1872.

Erected by ROBERT DONALD engineer Aberdeen in memory of his father PETER DONALD d.14
02 Dec.1847 aged 67 & his mother JANE TINDAL d.8 Mar.1868 aged 81. His eldest son ROBERT
d.Venice 26 June 1877 aged 24.

In loving memory of GEORGE LEES tailor d.2 May 1909 aged 29, ANDREW LEES d.20 Oct.1942
03 aged 36. (RHS) His wife GEORGINA STEPHEN d.Durban 14 Sept.1941 aged 63. (LHS) JEAN
LEES d.18 July 1987 wife of GORDON McGREGOR aged 84. Above GORDON McGREGOR d.5
Jan.1990 aged 90.

Erected by WILLIAM LEES fisherman Sketraw & ANN CHRISTIE his wife in memory of their dau.
ELIZABETH d.24 Sept.1880 aged 7mths., their son GEORGE d.20 Feb.1895 aged 16. Above
04 WILLIAM LEES d.31 May 1915 aged 61; above ANN CHRISTIE d.26 Feb.1930 aged 75. Their dau.
MAGGIE JANE d.22 Aug.1956 aged 69. Bottom: 4 lines verse. (Face now totally destroyed) (Shield)
In remembrance of MARY ANN CHRISTIE from her fellow workers.

In loving memory of ALEXA ANGUS wife of JOSEPH RITCHIE d.3 June 1900 aged 58. Their
family: MITCHELL d.23 June 1901 aged 19, SINA d.18 July 1906 aged 33, HERBERT d.1 May
05 1911 aged 35. Said JOSEPH RITCHIE d.9 June 1933 aged 85. WILLIAM d.Bournemouth 6 Mar.
1947 aged 80. ALEXA d.Benoni, S.A. 21 Apr.1952 aged 81; CHARLOTT (sic) d.London 13 Mar.
1955 aged 80, ANDREW d.there 18 Dec.1955 aged 87.

Erected by ANDREW ANGUS in affectionate remembrance of his wife HAMILTON
06 CRUICKSHANK d.13 Nov.1882 aged 67. His family: JOHN d.20 May 1859 aged 5, ELIZA d.11
Oct.1873 aged 34, JESSIE, ALEXANDER & HAMILTON all d.in infancy. Said ANDREW ANGUS
d.11 Oct.1899 aged 86. Bottom: Also his great grandchild HAMILTON BRUCE d.in infancy.

Erected by ALEXANDER ANGUS ship master in memory of his father ALEXANDER ANGUS d.5
Apr.1849 aged 39 & CHRISTIAN MITCHELL his wife d.Stonehaven 10 Feb.1865 aged 62. Above
07 Captn. ALEXANDER ANGUS d.14 Sept.1874 aged 44 & JANE LEES his wife d.28 Dec.1876 aged
44. Their dau.-in-law AGNES BERRY wife of ALEXR. ANGUS d.Montreal 2 Dec.1914 aged 44 &
is interred in Mount Royal Cemetery. Said ALEXANDER ANGUS watchmaker d.Stonehaven 5
Apr.1929 aged 63. His sister CHRISTINA d.8 Oct.1940.

---

08 In loving memory of our mother ISABELLA ANGUS d.5 Sept.1902 aged 69 & our father WILLIAM
RITCHIE d.6 Mar.1914 aged 78. Their dau. CHRISTINA MITCHELL d.14 June 1949 aged 82.

1765. AD. KW. Here lyes the body of ALEXANDER DEANS late smith in Couie d.ye 28 Mar.
09 1761 aged 72. Also his spouse KATHRINE WEBSTER d.17 Apr.1751 aged 69. Their son JAMES
DEANS d.ye 14 Oct.1758 aged 34; their dau. MARY DEANS d.28 June 1766 aged 51 & of their son
GEORGE DEANS once smith in Cowie d.20 May 1802 aged 88.

---

310 1818. In memory of JOHN BEATTIE late bleacher at Ury bleachfield d.17 June 1827 in 80th year also his spouse ELIZABETH CRAIG d.28 Mar.1817 in 70th year. Erected by her husband JOHN BEATTIE. (Back) In memory of their son WILLIAM BEATTIE Bridge of Cowie d.28 Jan.1860 aged 86.

---

311 DC. ID. 1717. (Back) (2 halves) (LS) Here lyes ane honest & wertwovs man DAVID CRAIG who lived in Cowie & dep.25 July 1742 of age 72. (RS) Here lyes ane honest and wertwovs woman JANET DEANS spows to DAVID CRAIG who dep.26 July 1700 of aged 60 years. (All spellings as on stone)

---

312 GEORGE ADAM pilot d.27 Apr.1903 aged 85 also CATHARINE GRAY his wife d.2 Sept.1920 aged 88.

---

313 Erected by GEORGE ADAM in memory of his father JAMES ADAM shipmaster d.Aberdeen 6 Oct.1887 aged 72 & his mother ISABELLA ANDERSON d.Stonehaven 18 Oct.1850 aged 36. His brother ROBERT ADAM lost at sea 26 Oct.1859 aged 17, his sister ANN d.20 Apr.1886 aged 40. His brother JAMES shipmaster d.28 Dec.1900 aged 60, his sister ISABEL d.26 Sept.1912 aged 67. Said GEORGE ADAM d.Aberdeen 1 June 1919 aged 70.

---

314 1778. DA. IN. Here lyes the body of DAVID ADAMS late seaman in Cowie d.6 Nov.1766 aged 47. (space) and of their children MARY, ANDREW, CHRISTIAN & ISABEL also JOHN & GEORGE.

---

315 RD. 1794. JS. We, the remaining friends erected this in memory of ROBERT DONALD d.30 May 1783 aged 82. His wife JANET SADLYOR d.7 Mar.1792 aged 84; their dau.CHRISTIAN d.10 Apr.1792 aged 36.

---

316 1848. TM. JL. In memory of THOMAS MITCHELL weaver Stonehaven d.8 Mar.1848 aged 43; his wife JANE LEES d.27 July 1888 aged 81. Of their children JAMES MITCHELL mariner d.off Cape Horn 2 July 1848 aged 18, ANDREW d.at sea 1 May 1861 aged 23, ALEXANDER slater d.1 Feb. 1862 aged 18 & THOMAS seaman d.Beathella Bay, Figi (sic) Islands 2 Oct.1881 aged 45.

---

317 Erected by JOHN MITCHELL weaver Stonehaven in memory of his family: MARY ANN d.12 June 1855 aged 5, CHARLES d.10 June 1859 aged 8, ROSINA d.30 Apr.1862 aged 15, PETER d.at sea 8 Sept.1877 aged 34 & was interred in an English Cemetery at Lishma, East Indies & JOHN d.in infancy. ROBERT ship master d.7 Jan.1881 aged 45; his wife MARY ANN ELDER COCHER d.6 June 1889 aged 68. His son JAMES d.Port Augusta, S.A. 11 Feb.1892 aged 51. His dau. MARGARET d.18 Jan.1895 aged 39. Above JOHN MITCHELL d.26 Oct.1895 aged 77.

---

318 M. In loving memory of JAMES MASSON 27 Skateraw Road, Newtonhill d.24 Feb.1976 aged 77. JOHN MASSON d.29 Aug.1993 aged 90 beloved husband of MARY MacGREGOR d.30 Apr.1996 aged 92.

---

319 Erected by JOHN CHRISTIE fisherman Sketrow in loving memory of his wife ISABELLA CHRISTIE d.3 Sept.1906 aged 69. Their son JAMES was lost at sea 15 Sept.1901 aged 37. Said JOHN CHRISTIE d.24 July 1913 aged 71. Their son PETER husband of MARGARET WOOD d.1 Dec.1938 aged 66; above MARGARET WOOD d.7 Dec.1951 aged 76.

---

320 In loving memory of ANN WHITTARD-BARRET d.18 Mar.1905 aged 65.

---

21   Erected by MARY MASSON in loving memory of her husband ROBERT CHRISTIE d.Torry 3 Nov.
1902 aged 42; above MARY MASSON d.23 Oct.1933 aged 72.

Erected by ALEXANDER LEES in loving memory of his wife ISABELLA McKECHNIE d.23 July
1902 aged 46. His son ALEXANDER lost at sea 17 Apr.1907 aged 27. 2 lines verse. His son
22   GEORGE d.Loyalist, Alberta, Canada 1 Feb.1921 aged 38. JAMES son of ALEXANDER & JANE
LEES d.23 Feb.1928 aged 22. Said ALEXANDER LEES d.28 Oct.1928 aged 72; his son ANDREW
d.Canada 28 Oct.1929 aged 32. Said JANE LEES d.20 Oct.1945 aged 78.

(Flat) (LHS) JB. Here lyes JAMES BURNET who lived in Blackbutts & d.2 Nov.1734 being of age
23   44. (RHS) JL. Also his spouse JANNET LIGHTON she d.2 June 1770 aged 81. Their son ANDREU
BURNET late Subtenant in Grains d.the 9th day of Jan.1775 aged 49. Also their dau. ISOBELL
BURNET d.2 Oct.1752 aged 33.

---

24   (Face mostly gone) Erected by/........MOWAT/.....of his wife/.....DUNCAN/48 years/....1881 years.

Sacred to the memory of JANE DONALDSON wife of JOHN GLASS tailor d.28 Apr.1893 aged 33.
25   Of their family NELLIE d.22 Feb.1894 aged 1, THOMAS d.26 Mar.1901 aged 18. Said JOHN
GLASS d.24 Aug.1909 aged 51. MAGGIE d.9 Nov.1909 aged 18. Bottom: Also his mother ANN
DAVIDSON d.27 Mar.1906 aged 80.

---

26   (Book) MAGGIE aged 18 - from her schoolmates Nov.1909.

---

27   Erected by HELEN ADAM in memory of her father & mother ANDREW ADAM d.28 Aug.1872
aged 67; AGNES SCORGIE d.14 Aug.1875 aged 67.

Erected by JAMES LEES fisherman Sketraw & JANE CHRISTIE his wife in loving memory of their
family JOHN d.28 Dec.1886 aged 7, ALEXANDER d.7 Jan.1887 aged 9, ROBERT d.21 Jan.1887
aged 2. Above JANE CHRISTIE d.14 June 1898 aged 47; above JAMES LEES d.17 Jan.1923 aged
28   74. Their son JAMES d.5 Sept.1941 aged 65; ELIZABETH BURNETT his wife d.8 Oct.1957 aged
85. Base: 2 lines verse. (Square in front) CECIL LEES SIMPSON great grandson d.16 July 1971
aged 46, JAMES BURNETT LEES grandson d.1 Oct.1981 aged 75. MARY ANABELLA LEES
grand-dau. d.21 July 1990 aged 76, JANE ANN FYFE LEES grand-dau. d.2 July 1996 aged 96.

---

29   In loving memory of GEORGE CHRISTIE d.17 July 1951 aged 75; his wife CHRISTINA LEES d.16
Apr.1936 aged 54. Their dau. MARGARET d.28 Sept.1986 aged 75.

Erected in memory of WILLIAM REITH late farmer Floors, Muchalls d.12 Apr.1862 aged 45. His
family WILLIAM d.24 Mar.1854 aged 4, WILLIAM CUSHNIE d.27 June 1876 aged 15. His wife
ELIZABETH ANDERSON d.10 Mar.1900 aged 72. Their dau. ELIZABETH wife of DAVID
30   STRACHAN late farmer Floors, Muchalls d.4 Oct.1916 aged 65. Bottom: His grandchildren
DAVID STRACHAN d.7 Jan.1867 aged 4 weeks, HUGH STRACHAN d.28 Feb.1872 aged 3mths.,
WILLIAM REITH STRACHAN d.6 July 1902 aged 33, DUNCAN L.M.STRACHAN fell in action
at Festubert, France 15 May 1915 aged 22.

In memory of HUGH STRACHAN farmer Floors, Muchalls d.28 Aug.1891 aged 80 & of his wife
ELIZABETH ANDERSON d.10 Mar.1900 aged 72. Of their family HUGH d.Johannesburg, S.A. 9
31   May 1904 aged 40, DAVID late farmer Floors d.25 Jan.1921 aged 79 & JAMES MARSHALL twin
brother of said HUGH d.Kensington 10 June 1929 aged 64. (Heart) JM. Our father.

---

332 1820. In memory of GEORGE KNOWLES d.Wester Logie 19 Jan.1838 aged 67; his spouse CHRISTIAN MILNE d.19 Mar.1849 & MARGARET dau. of GEORGE KNOWLES tenant in Stoneyhill d.1 Oct.1819 aged 15. His son GEORGE late farmer South Glenton d.Stonehaven 20 Oct. 1891 aged 86 & ELIZABETH SHERET his wife d.24 Nov.1892 aged 85.

---

333 1831. WR. AH. In memory of WILLIAM ROBB farmer Wellheads of Newhall d.4 Apr.1851 aged 83 & AMELIA HOGG his wife d.28 June 1808 aged 38. Of their children JEAN d.23 Jan.1819 aged 18, CHRISTIAN d.6 Nov.1820 aged 15, MARGARET d.8 Sept.1823 aged 26 & ELISABETH d.19 Oct.1861 aged 55. WILLIAM d.England, Portlethen 19 Feb.1887 aged 83, AGNES d.there 17 Feb. 1888 aged 86.

---

334 In memory of JOSEPH SPARK d.Windford 21 June 1888 aged 84; his wife MARGARET COLLIE d.21 Nov.1899 aged 76. Of their family JOHN ALEXANDER d.in infancy 1847, JANE d.28 Sept. 1859 aged 11mths., ANN d.25 Feb.1873 aged 22, ELIZA d.9 Jan.1924 aged 63. Their grandchild JOSEPH SPARK LEASK d.in infancy 1871. (Back) 1829. JK. MM. In memory of JOHN KNOWLES late tenant in Swineward of Barras d.1 Dec.1833 aged 67 & MARY MURRAY his wife d.9 Mar.1827 aged 37. Of their children WILLIAM d.3 Jan.1828 aged 5yrs 3mths., GEORGE d.in June 1841 aged 14.

---

335 1789. WK. Here lies the body of WILLIAM KNOWLES late tenant in Hillhead of Muchals (sic) d.8 Mar.1789 aged 90.

---

336 1864. In memory of ELIZABETH BAIN wife of JAMES GREIG merchant Stonehaven d.13 Aug. 1864 aged 62 & of their children JOHN & JAMES who d.in infancy, BENJAMIN d.7 July 1839 in 2nd year, MARY d.19 Dec.1874 aged 32. Above JAMES GREIG d.1 Feb.1881 aged 75.

---

337 1858. To the memory of GEORGE BAIN farmer in Readykes (sic) d.14 Mar.1858 aged 63; MARGARET ALLAN his wife d.23 Sept.1877 aged 86. Of their family ELISABETH d.18 Nov.1862 aged 30, MARY d.13 Apr.1864 aged 28 & COSMA (sic) GRANT their nephew d.13 May 1863 aged 9. ANN GRANT wife of GEORGE BAIN farmer Smallburn d.29 Dec.1888 aged 62; said GEORGE BAIN d.Laurencekirk 26 June 1914 aged 74. (Back) 1824. In memory of JOHN BAIN farmer in Causyside, Parish of Nether Banchory d.28 Jan.1810 aged 50; CHRISTIAN ROBB his spouse d.19 Oct.1823 aged 62. Of their children JOHN d.13 Aug.1818 aged 22 & BENJAMIN d.Ternate Island 5 Dec.1822 aged 33.

---

338 1832. AM. JC. In memory of ALEXANDER MASSON seaman in Sketraw d.5 Apr.1787 aged 61; JANET CHRISTIE his wife d.29 Jan.1822 aged 83. Of their children ALEXANDER d.22 Sept.1815 aged 41, ANDREW d.10 Jan.1832 aged 63, MARGARET d.18 Dec.1836 aged 68, ELSPET d.27 Feb.1843 aged 67, ISOBEL d.17 Oct.1849 aged 67. (Back) JM. MW. In memory of JAMES MASSON d.Cowie 6 June 1835 aged 55; MARY WATT his wife d.28 Sept.1824 aged 34. Of their children JAMES d.in infancy, MARY d.8 June 1844 aged 28, ALEXANDER d.14 Sept.1861 aged 41, ANDREW d.7 Mar.1879 aged 65, JAMES d.2 Feb.1883 aged 58.

---

339 Erected by CHRISTINA MASSON in affectionate remembrance of her husband ALEXANDER LEIPER d.17 May 1875 aged 51. Of their family ISABELLA d.7 Feb.1852 aged 10 weeks, JAMES MASSON d.30 July 1861 aged 8, ALEXANDER d.23 May 1863 aged 4. Above CHRISTINA MASSON d.26 Feb.1903 aged 74. Bottom: 2 lines verse.

---

340 Erected by his family in loving remembrance of their father DONALD McINNES who was accidentally killed on the railway at Muchalls 30 Apr.1881 aged 56; his son DONALD d.20 Sept./

40   /1875 aged 3mths. His wife MARGARET WALKER d.Muchalls 21 Apr.1917 aged 81. His dau.
ont   ISABELLA d.19 Dec.1924 aged 67. Bottom: KENNETH brother of DONALD McINNES who was
      killed on the railway at (Fetteresso) Cutting 14 Nov.1878 aged 45.

      In loving memory of AGNES ANN DORIAN wife of THRIFT WATT saddler d.25 Aug.1903 aged
41   62. Their son ALEXANDER d.11 Nov.1909 aged 37; their grandson GEORGE WATT killed in
      action at Gallipoli 26 June 1915 aged 37.

      Erected by JOSEPH CHALMERS East Backburn, Ury in memory of his wife ELIZABETH
42   JAMIESON d.4 Nov.1875 aged 49; said JOSEPH CHALMERS d.Greenheads, Muchalls 16 Feb.
      1896 aged 75. Their daus. ISABELLA d.20 Feb.1923 aged 58, MARY d.17 Jan.1952 aged 85.

      In loving memory of WILLIAM CHALMERS d.Stonehaven 22 Jan.1904 aged 76; HELEN
      MIDDLETON his wife d.6 June 1909 aged 81. Of their family DAVID d.West Blackbutts, Muchalls
43   20 Mar.1910 aged 59, ANDREW d.in Hawaiian Isles 7 Mar.1910 aged 42. Their son-on-law
      CHARLES W.B.HAY d.Stonehaven 17 June 1901. ALICE JOHNSON wife of above DAVID
      CHALMERS (no date given). WILLIAM CHALMERS son of DAVID & ALICE d.West Blackbutts
      21 July 1955 aged 75 & his wife BARBARA KEITH d.Druidsdale, Barras 2 Aug.1977 aged 87.

      1778. DM. SC. Here lyes SARAH CORMOCK wife of DAVID MIDDELTON (left side gone)
44   d.10 July 1780 aged 8-. (This stone) was erected by DAVID MIDDELTON in Couie in memory of
      his dau. MARGARET ? d.7........1770 in infancy also his son DAVID he d.1 Nov.1778 aged 16.
      (Face now gone)

      In loving memory of DAVID SUTHERLAND d.6 Jan.1889 aged 62 & his wife MARY
45   ROBERTSON d.13 May 1908 aged 73. Their dau. MARY d.21 Mar.1888 aged 24. (Most of this
      now gone).

----

46   (Face mostly gone) Erected by HELE..../in memory of/ALEX(ANDER)....../fish...../ Rest gone.

      (Flat -inside church) Diptych. (LHS) IN. IN. Here lies the body of JOHN NEPER late seaman in
47   Muchall dep.28 Mar.1766 aged 90. (RHS) Hereunder lyeth JEAN NEPER spous to JOHN NEPER
      in Seatoun of Muchels (sic) dep.15 Jan.1717 & of her aged 30.

----

48   (On wall) Erected by ANN CHRISTIE in memory of her husband ALEXANDER MASSON late
      farmer? in Cairngrassie ....22 Mar.1856 aged 51. The said.........(rest of face gone)

      (Table) To the memory of MARY SEATON d.18 June 1815 aged 74?. This stone is erected by
49   JOHN INNES of Cowie in whose family she served faithfully & affectionately for nearly half a
      century.

      Erected by GEORGE WATT tinsmith in loving memory of his wife ANN LINDSAY d.25 Apr.1884
      aged 54; said GEORGE WATT d.16 July 1896 aged 66. JANE ANN his dau. & widow of WILLIAM
0   MURRAY d.28 May 1929 in 64th year. Their son GEORGE WATT d.27 Sept.1932 aged 71.
      WILLIAMINA HAMILTON MURRAY dau. of above WILLIAM MURRAY d.29 June 1937 aged
      43.

      Erected by GEORGE & MARGARET WATT in memory of their parents JANE STRACHAN d.15
1   Feb.1855 aged 55 & DANIEL WATT shoemaker Stonehaven d.27 June 1871 aged 78. Said
      MARGARET WATT d.3 Apr.1898 aged 70. Bottom: 2 lines verse.

352   1848. Erected by MOSES CADENHEAD farmer Achlea of Kingcausie in memory of his wife CHRISTIAN BAIN d.23 Feb.1847 aged 51. His sister MARY CADENHEAD d.26 June 1865 aged 67; above MOSES CADENHEAD d.25 Aug.1876 aged 81.

---

353   In memory of JEAN INNES d.26 June 1831 aged 82.

---

354   Here rests JOHN INNES formerly of Leuchars & for many years Sheriff Substitute of this County d.10 May 1827 in 80th year.

---

355   Erected by her parents to the beloved remembrance of BETSY D. McLEAN d.12 May 1844 aged 13. Deeply regretted. The burial place of WILLIAM McLEAN. (Now broken, in two parts)

---

356   In memory of FRANCIS O. HUNT 1904-1965. (Square in front) CC.

---

357   Erected by WILLIAM KEITH Hillside Muchalls in memory of his wife MARY SPARK d.14 July 1901 aged 83; said WILLIAM KEITH d.17 Jan.1916 aged 90. Of their family ALEXANDER d.20 Nov.1851 aged 1, JOHN d.13 Nov.1892 aged 40.

---

358   1823. To the memory of ALEXR. WYLLIE wright d.Cantla-hills 7 Aug. aged 42. Their son JOSEPH d.10 Oct.1875 aged 56. Of their childern (sic) JANE d.8 Aug.1823 aged 11, JOHN d.3 Mar. 1824 aged 10, ALEXR. d.28 Mar.1824 aged 9. His wife HANNAH SPARK d.20 Mar.1849 aged 68. (Back) Sacred to the memory of HANNAH SPARK wife of GEORGE SPARK junr. farmer Badens d.23 Jan.1852 aged 35 & of their infant son JOHN aged 2 days who d.the same day as his mother. Above GEORGE SPARK d.29 Sept.1896 aged 76 & ANN GORDON his 2nd wife d.4 Feb.1899 aged 83.

---

359   (Table) Sacred to the memory of PETER LOGIE d.14 Sept.1765 aged 50; his wife CHRISTIAN MITCHELL d.24 Mar.1807 aged 82. Their son-in-law JAMES JOHNSTON d.27 Oct.1824 aged 70; his wife CHRISTIAN LOGIE d.20 Dec.1846 in 93rd year. Their youngest dau. MARY JOHNSTON d.24 Feb.1849 aged 57.

---

360   (Table) Here lie interred WILLIAM MIDDLETON baker in Stonehaven d.5 June 1774 aged 64 & ISOBEL MEARNS his 2nd wife d.in 1812 aged 86. Their children JOHN, JANET, MARGARET, ANN, ISOBEL & HELEN who all d.in their youth.

---

361   In memory of JOHN BRIDGEFORD late tenant in Glenton d.16 Aug.1782 aged 67; his spouse MARY MAIN d.in 1806 aged 97. Of their children GEORGE, JOHN, ALEXR, WILLIAM, ROBERT & ISOBEL. THOMAS BRIDGEFORD d.27 Apr.1825 aged 84 & his spouse ELIZABETH DURRIE d.10 Feb.1808 & his dau. ELSPIT d.6 Nov.1817 aged 14.

---

362   Erected by JAMES CARNEGIE pilot in memory of his children JESSIE d.26 Sept.1878 aged 7, WILLIAM d.in infancy 8 May 1882. Above JAMES CARNEGIE d.23 Apr.1916 aged 69; his wife ROSE STOTT d.28 June 1929 aged 80.

---

363   (Face mostly gone) 1799 GK AM (In memo)ry of........./...........Tenant in/.........d.Nov.the/........... years also/A.............M..........N his EsPous/w...Decr.the 29 1792/aged 72 ....lso their son JA... .....une the 3 1771/...............also five of their/..............ied in infency.....(rest gone) (Back) In memory of ADAM CHARLES Dyer Stonehaven d.6 Jan.1844 aged 62 & ANN DONALD his wife d.10 May 1833 aged 50.   His great grandson JOHN MAXWELL TAYLOR M.A.,M.B.,Ch.B., D.P.H., d.11 Feb.1965 aged 88 & his wife ALICE DUNCAN d.3 Mar.1971 aged 81.

53a   Fallen face down.

1808. To the memory of WILLIAM DONALD mason in Links of Arduthie d.24 June 1816 in 67th year; his spouse ELSPET KEITH d.17 Sept.1807 aged 57. Of their children JOHN, AGNUS (sic) & JAMES who d.in infancy. ELSPET SMITH 2nd wife of WILLIAM DONALD d.3 Dec.1868 aged 80. (Back) And to the memory of WILLIAM SMITH mason in Aberdeen d.4 Jan.1853 aged 88; ELSPET DONALD his wife d.7 Aug.1868 aged 87. Their youngest dau.CHRISTINA d.Aberdeen 20 Oct.1889 aged 66.

54

----

55   Erected by ALEXANDER JACKSON brewer in Johnshaven in memory of his wife JANET DONALD d.27 Oct.1837 aged 47.

1828. JC. MA. In memory of JAMES CARNEGIE farmer in Middle Toucks d.16 Feb.1854 aged 71; MARGARET ADAM his wife d.2 June 1831 aged 51. Of their children MARGARET d.23 Nov. 1822 aged 15. (Back) In memory of JAMES CARNEGIE once tenant in Arduthie d.11 Mar. 1805 aged 70; ISOBEL HOWIE his wife d.in Apr.1836 aged 96.

56

1885. Erected by JAMES CARNEGIE formerly tenant in Toucks, Dunnottar & CATHERINE SMITH his wife in loving memory of their family: HUGH d.in infancy 1855, DAVID d.22 Nov.1862 aged 4, WILLIAM d.20 July 1865 aged 1. Above JAMES CARNEGIE who for 40 years was tenant in Toucks d.Union Cottage, Rickarton 6 Dec.1890 aged 78. Above CATHERINE SMITH d.Ayr.19 Feb.1908 aged 85 - interred here. Also their son JAMES d.17 Feb.1922 aged 70 - interred in Broomhill Cemetery. Their dau.CATHERINE d.Ayr.13 June 1926 aged 70 - interred here. Their son JOHN d.Kimberley Cottage, Nigg 18 Apr.1936 aged 74 - interred here.

57

----

58   (Celtic Cross) Erected in memory of ANN CHARLES d.11 Dec.1902 aged 81.

----

59   In memory of SUSAN CONSTANCE HASSELL widow of WILLIAM HASSELL of Bristol d.4 Aug. 1906.

In loving memory of JOHN MILLER younger son of WILLIAM CROWLEY bank agent b.Lochee 5 May 1926, accidentally killed at Wishaw 7 Sept.1931. 4 lines verse. Base: WILLIAM PETER elder son b.Newburgh-on-Tay 23 Aug.1922 - d.Perth 9 Oct.1935.

60

Sacred to the memory of Revd. PETER BROWN CROWLEY M.A. for 50 years beloved & devoted minister in Stonehaven d.North Manse 14 May 1936 aged 79; his wife JESSIE MANN d.17 Mar. 1945 aged 78. His dau.BEATRICE JESSIE d.11 Jan.1961 aged 60; his niece ELIZABETH KINNEAR d.5 Jan.1964 aged 73. His son WILLIAM d.30 Mar.1966 aged 73 also wife of above, MARY T.M.CROWLEY d.6 Nov.1984 aged 87.

61

----

62   In loving memory of JEANNIE CROWLEY b.11 June 1895 - d.2 Dec.1897, elder dau. of Rev. P.B. CROWLEY.

In memory of MARY SOUTTAR wife of JOHN GRAY McKENDRICK M.D. Professor of Physiology in the University of Glasgow b.16 Jan.1842 - d.18 Nov.1898. WILLIAM JAMES McKENDRICK B.Sc., M.B. their eldest son d.& was interred at Prince Albert, Cape of Good Hope - b.17 May 1868 - d.23 Apr.1892. Above JOHN GRAY McKENDRICK M.D.,LL.D.,F.R.S. b.12 Aug. 1841 - d.2 Jan.1926.

63

----

374   In memory of HELEN JANE WELSH wife of GEORGE MURRAY F.R.S. Keeper of Botany, British Museum d.19 Oct.1902. GEORGE MURRAY F.R.S. d.Stonehaven 16 Dec.1911.

In loving memory of GEORGE SCOTT CAIRD solicitor Stonehaven, Procurator Fiscal of
375   Kincardineshire b.2 Sept.1828 - d.14 Sept.1897. His wife CHRISTIAN SHARPE d.Northam, North Devon 10 Dec.1904 aged 72. Their sons GEORGE CHARLES d.10 Feb.1922 aged 57, ALEXANDER SHARPE d.11 June 1926 aged 60.

1901. WILHELMINA LESLIE SOUTTAR wife of SIDNEY HERBERT of the Stock Exchange,
376   London d.Stonehaven 10 Sept.1901 aged 32. (Round plaque) In loving & honoured memory of HUGH LESLIE HERBERT Lieut.8th Bn.Gordon Hlrs. killed in action Festubert, France 7 Aug.1915 aged 19. Text.

Erected by JOHN SPARK Broomhill, Muchalls in memory of his wife AGNES ROBERTSON d.29
377   July 1873 aged 50. His family: ANN d.2 May 1856 aged 3, JAMES d.3 Apr.1866 aged 4mths. Above JOHN SPARK d.Hawthorn Cottage, Muchalls 2 Feb.1904 aged 82; ELIZABETH SCOTT his 2nd wife d.11 July 1916 aged 82.

In loving memory of CHARLES CHRISTIE 2nd son of Very Rev. WM. CHRISTIE Dean of Moray d.Stonehaven 12 Aug.1893 aged 32; 3rd son ROBERT EDEN CHRISTIE d.Winchester 5 June 1906
378   aged 43 - both interred here. His eldest son Very Rev. WILLIAM LESLIE CHRISTIE Dean of Brechin, Incumbent of St. James' Church for 41 years d.27 Jan.1931 aged 72 & his wife MARGARET ASHMORE CHRISTIE d.22 Dec.1944 aged 85.

Erected by DAVID CHALMERS Greenheads, Muchalls in memory of his wife JOANNA
379   FARQUHAR d.23 May 1902 aged 41; their infant son JOHN ALEXANDER d.10 June 1902. His 2nd wife ANNIE DUNCAN d.9 June 1935 aged 75; said DAVID CHALMERS d.21 Nov.1935 aged 84.

----

380   In memory of WILLIAM STEPHEN shipmaster b.Fraserburgh 6 Oct.1845 - d.Stonehaven 15 Mar. 1908. His wife FANNY M. HIGHBY d.Stonehaven 4 Aug.1946 aged 92.

----

381   In loving memory of JAMES GORHAM retired Chief Boatman, H.M. Coastguards d.17 Mar.1911 aged 70.

----

382   Pray for the soul of the Rev. JAMES STEWART who for 18 years administered to the spiritual wants of the Catholics of Stonehaven d.1 June 1899. 1 line text.

----

383   JOHN SOUTTAR b.Peterhead 8 Aug.1836 - d.Stonehaven 27 May 1910. 1 line text.

----

384   Sacred to the memory of MAY dau. of WILLIAM SMYTH writer Glasgow b.25 Mar.1833 - d.12 July 1912. 2 lines text.

----

385   Erected in memory of our mother ELSIE PROCTOR McDONALD d.28 Apr.1900 aged 52.

Erected by JAMES TAYLOR in loving memory of his wife MARGARET INGRAM d.30 Dec.1930
386   aged 67. Of their family: JESSIE ANN d.Winnipeg 12 Jan.1920 aged 33, LIZZIE & HARRY d.in infancy. Above JAMES TAYLOR late farmer Wester Logie d.Dundee 7 Mar.1932 aged 70. (Under) In loving memory of LIZZIE TAYLOR d.Wester Logie, Stonehaven 12 Jan.1900 aged 6mths.

----

87 Erected by MARY CHRISTIE in loving memory of her husband JOHN CHRISTIE fisherman Skateraw d.10 July 1928 aged 62; their dau. MARY d.in infancy 1898. Above MARY CHRISTIE d.13 Sept.1933 aged 69. 1 line text. (Heart under) JC. In memory of little MARY d.2 Dec.1898.

----

88 In loving memory of JOHN ROBERT HUTCHEON d.11 July 1901 aged 2½. His father ALEXANDER HUTCHEON d.7 Dec.1947 aged 84; his mother MARY TAYLOR d.15 May 1952 aged 83.

----

89 Erected by ALEXR. KEITH in memory of his son DAVID d.Broomhill, Muchalls 20 Feb.1898 aged 2yrs 7mths. His wife MARGARET MESTON d.15 Feb.1935 aged 82; said ALEXANDER KEITH d.13 Dec.1935 aged 78. HELEN SHEPHERD wife of JAMES A.KEITH d.13 Dec.1956 aged 64. JAMES ALEXANDER KEITH husband of above, late of Hillocks, Muchalls d.Cowie 26 Aug.1960 aged 69.

----

90 In memory of our mother MAGGIE FORREST wife of GEORGE W.KEITH shipmaster d.30 Dec. 1913 aged 52; our father the above GEORGE W.KEITH d.3 Mar.1941 aged 83. Our sisters MAGGIE KEITH d.Hull 14 Jan.1953 aged 64, ISABELLA CAMERON KEITH d.Kirkella, Hull 10 Sept.1958 aged 63.

----

91 In memory of JOHN GLASS d.15 Jan.1941 aged 60; his wife HELEN TAYLOR MURRAY d.24 Jan.1956 aged 79. Their son STANLEY d.14 Mar.1983, husband of MARGARITA GAMMIE. (Embossed heart) In loving memory of MARGARITA GLASS (SPANKIE) aged 2½.

----

92 In loving memory of our father JAMES CHALMERS d.18 Apr.1918, our mother JESSIE STEPHEN d.24 Nov.1903 also our brother & sister interred here.

----

93 In remembrance of JAMES CHALMERS retired postman d.2 June 1939 aged 80. Of his family DANIEL FISHER d.17 Feb.1895 aged 4, ROYCE ARCHIBALD d.24 Nov.1907 aged 8mths. ESTHER CORMIE his wife d.10 July 1941 aged 78. BARBARA their 2nd dau. d.21 Nov.1956 aged 62 - interred in Fetteresso Cemetery. ROBERT S. their 2nd son d.14 Oct.1957 aged 70.

----

94 Erected by JAMES & GEORGE TAYLOR in memory of their aunt CATHERINE MILNE merchant Newtonhill d.2 Jan.1899 aged 72.

----

95 In loving memory of DAVID KEITH farmer Hillside, Muchalls d.2 May 1925 aged 64; his wife BARBARA McDONALD CRAIG d.Mosside, Portlethen 29 Jan.1957 aged 90. Also of his family JOHN & ANNIE who d.in infancy.

----

96 In memory of DAVID COBB b.11 Oct.1882 - d.12 May 1896.

----

97 In loving memory of DAVID PORTER tailor d.26 Sept.1927 aged 68; his dau. HENRIETTA d.21Jan.1898 aged 2. His wife EDITH CADENHEAD d.10 Feb.1932 aged 71. (Heart) Wee ETTA 1898.

----

98 In loving memory of ALEXANDER MORRICE FIDDES b.1 Feb.1861 - d.29 July 1933; his wife ALEXANDERINA B. GORDON b.25 Mar.1864 - d.26 Feb.1944. Their son-in-law BERTRAM GEORGE SAWER b.11 Apr.1886 - d.3 Feb.1952. ETHEL MARY FIDDES d.2 Jan.1970 aged 74, her sister JESSIE ISABELLA FIDDES d.17 July 1972 aged 80.

----

399   In loving memory of JOHN STEPHEN tailor d.26 Nov.1930 aged 67; his sons DAVID d.in infancy, WILLIAM d.5 May 1910 aged 6½. His wife MARGARET DUFF d.25 Jan.1937 aged 67. Their dau. MARY MORRIS d.5 July 1983 aged 82. Their grandson JACK STEPHEN b.2 Oct.1913 - d.23 Nov. 1996. (Now face down)

400   Erected by ALEXR. KNOX in loving memory of his son ALEXANDER d.Royal Infirmary 12 Dec. 1898 aged 20. His grandson ALEXANDER who was accidentally killed at Stonehaven Ry. Station 21 Oct.1899 aged 6½. Said ALEXr. KNOX d.1 Dec.1909 aged 58; his wife ISABELLA GOODBRAND d.16 Oct.1930 aged 78. His dau. MARY MURDOCH d.2 Apr.1970 aged 82.

401   Erected by JAMES DONALDSON Officer of Fisheries in loving memory of his wife HELEN KINNEAR ALLARDYCE d.Campbeltown 5 Apr.1899 aged 40. JAMES DONALDSON d.14 Apr.1922 aged 64. His dau. MARJORY MITCHELL d.28 Dec.1934 aged 32. 1 line text.

402   In loving memory of FILOMENA ARCARI wife of FRANCESCO D'AGOSTINO d.31 Oct.1915 aged 48. Their son ANTHONY d.10 Jan.1961. (Shield) LUIGI D'AGOSTINO d.5 Feb.1896 aged 10mths.

403   Erected by WM. & HELEN ARCHIBALD in memory of their sons WILLIAM WALLACE d.Port Elizabeth, S.A. 1894 aged 26, JOHN d.Stonehaven 1895 aged 25, ALEXANDER d.1903 aged 30. Above WM. ARCHIBALD d.1914 aged 82; above HELEN ARCHIBALD d.1924 aged 83. (LHS) Also of ANNIE WALLACE sister-in-law d.1908 aged 57. Also of their dau. HELEN A. ARCHIBALD d.Stonehaven 11 Apr.1963 aged 85.

404   Erected in memory of JAMES BARRIE b.8 Apr.1843 - d.9 Aug.1918; his wife MARGARET MURDOCH BOWMAN b.2 Dec.1837 - d.11 June 1933. His daus. ANNIE FINDLAY BARRIE b.20 Oct.1869 - d.5 July 1899, JANET LOUISA BARRIE b.3 June 1881 - d.19 Mar.1943.

405   In memory of MARGARET HARDIE GEORGE wife of ALEXANDER ERNEST PHILIP GARDNER solicitor, Stonehaven d.5 May 1908; MARGARET their dau. d.in infancy. JOHN CLANACHAN GARDNER solicitor, Stonehaven their son d.5 July 1957; his wife JANE MAY LAWSON d.5 Aug.1965. (RHS) Also JULIA BEITH GARDNER dau. of first named d.29 Sept.1988.

406   (W.G.) 290524 Pte. F. MITCHELL Gordon Highlanders 18 July 1918.

407   Sacred to the memory of JOHN LESLIE late of Kingshill,Countesswells d.6 Nov.1901 aged 85; his son-in-law GEORGE CRICHTON blacksmith d.28 June 1928 aged 72. ISABELLA LESLIE wife of said GEORGE CRICHTON d.8 Apr.1948 aged 87.

408   In loving memory of our father WILLIAM DUNCAN d.3 Aug.1937 aged 79; his wife HELEN CHRISTIE d.22 Dec.1906 aged 47. Their dau. HELEN ANN d.in infancy; their grandchild JANE ANN BLAIR DUNCAN d.22 July 1909 aged 4. (Book) In memory of HELEN ANN DUNCAN aged 5mths. (Shield) In loving memory of our dear father.

409   In loving memory of DAVID KEMP Newtonhill d.21 Mar.1931 aged 69; his wife ANN TAYLOR d.8 Nov.1931 aged 70. Their son WILLIAM KEMP bank manager, Torphins d.8 June 1950 aged 57; his wife MARJORY GRAY d.24 Nov.1974 aged 80.

410   (Heart) Wee EMILY.

1 In loving memory of THOMAS McKANEY d.18 Oct.1895 aged 72; his wife JANE IVORY d.21 Apr.1899 aged 74. Of their family: ANN d.20 Feb.1912 aged 59, VIOLET d.24 Feb.1916 aged 45, JEANNIE d.1 June 1938 aged 74, JOHN d.21 Apr.1944 aged 85. Bottom: Erected by JOHN HUTCHEON.

----

2 In loving memory of CATHERINE ROSA younger dau. of ALEXANDER W. & ALICE M. HUNTER d.London 27 Sept.1934 aged 29. ALEXANDER WILLIAM HUNTER d.London 17 July 1944 aged 78; ALICE MARY MATTHEWS d.Hampshire 10 Jan.1951 aged 86. (Urn) In loving memory of my husband PETER CHRISTIE.

----

3 In loving memory of GEORGE DURWARD farmer Wellheads, Muchalls d.11 May 1898 aged 60; his wife MARY JANE LEASK d.Beachview, Stonehaven 2 Apr.1919 aged 69. Their dau. MARGARET CRAIB d.7 Apr.1944 aged 63. (Heart) In loving memory of GEORGE DURWARD.

----

4 In memory of EDWARD COLLIE d.22 Feb.1900; his wife AGNES MILNE d.26 July 1935 aged 85. Their family: MAGGIE d.in infancy, FRED killed in action 1916.

----

5 Erected by ELSPET ANDERSON in memory of her husband JOHN ANDERSON d.1 May 1900 aged 55. Their dau. MARGARET DURWARD d.1878 in infancy. Above ELSPET ANDERSON d.6 Apr.1929 aged 82. 1 line text.

----

6 Erected by JAMES CHRISTIE & ELSPET LEES his wife in loving memory of their family: MARGARET CRAIG d.31 Jan.1884 aged 1yr 8mths., MARGARET d.11 Dec.1888 aged 5mths., JAMES d.9 July 1896 aged 7mths., MARY d.25 Mar.1898 aged 20, ELSPET ANN d.19 Nov.1903 aged 26. Above JAMES CHRISTIE d.24 Dec.1918 aged 66, his wife ELSPET LEES d.20 Aug.1934 aged 82.

----

7 Erected by JAMES MOIR shipmaster in loving memory of his wife ANNABELLA d.2 Dec.1897 aged 56; above JAMES MOIR d.16 July 1924. Base: 2 lines text. (LHS) Their dau. MINA d.21 July 1956 aged 88.

----

8 Erected by JANE MAIN in loving memory of her husband ALEXANDER ADAMS fisherman d.30 July 1917 aged 63. Of their family: JAMES d.31 Dec.1908 aged 31, ROBERT & JESSIE d.in infancy. Above JANE MAIN d.18 Apr.1939 aged 84. Her parents MARGARET GIBB d.23 Sept. 1897 aged 71, JAMES MAIN d.4 Feb.1902 aged 79. 1 line motto.

----

9 (Heart) In loving remembrance of ROBERT MAIN d.5 Aug.1895 aged 4.

----

10 In memory of MAGGIE DUNBAR wife of JAMES C.BARCLAY druggist d.5 Feb.1908 aged 44; above JAMES C.BARCLAY d.St.Leonards, Stonehaven 30 Jan.1940 aged 74. MARGARETTA POWELL wife of above d.5 Nov.1957 aged 75. (RHS) Their son GORDON POWELL d.21 Jan.1962 aged 52. PEARL OSBORNE wife of Provost DAVID BARCLAY J.P.,M.B.,Ch.B.,D.P.H. d.8 Apr.1975 aged 58. The said Dr. DAVID BARCLAY J.P.,M.B.,Ch.B.,D.P.H. former Provost, Stonehaven d.10 Apr.1990 aged 77 beloved husband of MARGARET WILKINSON.

----

11 In memory of ROBERT BARCLAY shipmaster d.2 July 1896 aged 61; his wife ELIZABETH REITH d.10 July 1904 aged 66. Their eldest son ROBERT d.8 Jan.1924 aged 61. AGNES MITCHELL wife of ROBERT BARCLAY junr. d.21 Sept.1944 aged 80.

----

422   For King & Empire. In loving memory of ROBERT A.BARCLAY L/Cpl. 7th Gordon Highlanders, eldest son of W.BARCLAY, killed at Beaumont Hamel, France 13 Nov.1916 aged 20. Above WILLIAM BARCLAY d.20 May 1947 aged 79; his wife MARGARET WOOD d.5 July 1953 aged 84.

-----

423   In memory of ARTHUR WOOD shipmaster d.22 June 1897 aged 77.

-----

424   Erected by JAMES THOM in loving memory of his wife ANN NOBLE d.19 July 1927 aged 57; his dau. BESSIE d.8 July 1899 aged 3. Above JAMES THOM d.12 Jan.1944 aged 68.

-----

425   Erected by MARGARET MELVIN in loving memory of her husband JOHN GOODSMAN, H.M.Customs d.18 July 1899 aged 36. Said MARGARET MELVIN d.22 June 1925 aged 66.

-----

426   Erected by WILLIAM LEIPER in memory of his children JAMES & WILLIAM (twins) - JAMES d.4 Oct.1898 aged 9 mths., WILLIAM d.15 Sept.1899 aged 20 mths., ROSIE CARNEGIE d.11 Jan.1903 aged 6. His wife ROSE STOTT CARNEGIE d.25 May 1939 aged 65, above WILLIAM LEIPER d.11 Sept.1942 aged 70.

-----

427   In memory of ALEXANDER LEES shipmaster d.11 July 1897 aged 56; his wife JANE LEES d.14 Dec.1929 aged 84. His son JAMES drowned Cruden Scaurs 1 Mar.1902 aged 34.

-----

428   In loving memory of ALEXANDER LEES ship-master husband of MARY J.MITCHELL d.1 Sept. 1936 aged 68. Their children ALEXANDER aged 2½, JAMES aged 2½, CHARLES aged 13 mths. Above MARY J.MITCHELL d.12 Mar.1963 aged 92. Son-in-law ALEXANDER W.LAING husband of CONSTANCE d.23 May 1972 aged 66; their dau. CONSTANCE d.17 Sept.1978.

-----

429   Erected by ALEXANDER CHRISTIE & his wife ISABELLA CRAIG in memory of their family: ANDREW d.19 June 1880 aged 1, ARTHUR d.1890 aged 2 mths., JOHN d.at sea 30 Apr.1896 aged 20, WILLIAM d.Harwich 18 Mar.1916 aged 33. Above ISABELLA CRAIG d.14 Apr.1927 aged 78; ALEXANDER CHRISTIE d.17 Nov.1927 aged 77. (Now face down)

-----

430   (Shield) W.H.MARTIN S.O. A token of respect from H.M.Coastguard crews of Muchalls and Stonehaven 1903.

-----

431   (Heart) T.KENNY d.18 Oct.1895.

-----

432   Erected by GEORGE DAVIDSON in loving memory of his wife JANE CHRISTIE d.22 Aug.1902 aged 56; above GEORGE DAVIDSON d.31 May 1932 aged 78.

-----

433   In loving memory of JOHN FORBES GORDON d.25 Jan.1925 aged 71; his wife HELEN FINDLAY d.3 June 1936 aged 76 & their children MARY JESSIE & LESLIE.

-----

434   In loving memory of my husband GEORGE CALDER d.10 May 1898 aged 62; MARTHA GLENNIE wife of above d.22 June 1917 aged 72. Dau. JEANIE d.10 Jan.1952 aged 66. MARY ANN LEES wife of JAMES STRACHAN d.27 Apr.1941 aged 69; said JAMES STRACHAN d.8 June 1955 aged 89.

-----

435   Erected by JANE SHEWAN in memory of her husband JOHN CHAPMAN d.22 Nov.1899 aged 77; their son CHARLES d.Glasgow 18 June 1889 aged 37 & is interred in Paisley Cemetery. Dau. ISABELLA d.Glasgow 1 Mar.1903 aged 53 & is interred in Cathcart Cemetery. Said JANE/

5con./SHEWAN d.Glasgow 20 Dec.1915 aged 89 & interred Rutherglen Cemetery.

Erected by ALEXANDER CHRISTIE & CHRISTINA MASSON in memory of their son
6 ALEXANDER d.20 Mar.1903 aged 34. Said ALEXANDER CHRISTIE d.18 Nov.1904 aged 78;
CHRISTINA MASSON his wife d.26 Feb.1908 aged 79. 1 line text.

-----

7 Erected by ISABELLA & ELEANOR F. SEARCH in memory of their mother MARY RIDDELL d.
Sukkur, India 13 Aug.1879 aged 48. Their aunt ELEANOR RIDDELL d.Cowie 7 Dec.1899 aged 74.

Erected by ISABELLA MASSON in loving memory of her husband JOSEPH CHRISTIE
accidentally drowned in the channel Aberdeen 28 Jan.1911 aged 57. Dau. JANE M. CHRISTIE
8 d.1897 aged 1yr 9 mths., son WILLIAM fell in action near Loos, France 25 Sept.1915 aged 30.
Above ISABELLA MASSON d.3 Feb.1917 aged 57. Bottom: Their grandchild ALICE CHRISTIE
d.10 Feb.1915 aged 4mths.

Erected by ALEXANDER ADAM & CHRISTINA LEES his wife in loving memory of their family:
9 JOHN d.29 Oct.1921 aged 23, ALEXANDER & JANE d.in infancy, ROBERT d.8 July 1923 aged
4½, ADAM d.21 Apr.1934 aged 17. Above ALEXANDER ADAM d.21 Feb.1946 aged 70; above
CHRISTINA LEES d.14 Nov.1957 aged 82. (Vase) ADAM Father & Mother.

Erected by HELEN MASSON in loving memory of her husband JAMES LEIPER d.19 Aug.1933
0 aged 86. Above HELEN MASSON d.2 Apr.1936 aged 85. (Book) In memory of a dear son JOHN
LEIPER d.7 July 1894 aged 4yrs 6mths. Verse.

0a (Heart) In memory of our 4 children who d.in infancy. J.REID

Erected by GEORGE LEES in loving memory of his wife ELIZABETH MORRICE d.28 Mar.1893
1 aged 38; said GEORGE LEES d.22 Aug.1905 aged 53. His 2nd wife JESSIE CRAIG d.18 Sept.1913
aged 51.

Erected by JANE LEIPER in loving memory of her husband GEORGE McKECHNIE d.14 Apr.1909
2 aged 46. Of her children JANE ANN & ELSIE d.in infancy, JOHN her son d.9 Nov.1941 aged 54.
Above JANE LEIPER d.26 Aug.1944 aged 82. Bottom: Her nephew Pte. JOHN RUSSEL 5th
Gordon Highlanders d.of wounds 12 May 1917 aged 21. (Bottom part now gone)

-----

3 (Shield) In memory of WILLIAM ADAM aged 38 also his family MAGGIE aged 21; WILLIAM
aged 11; BELLA aged 3½.

-----

4 In loving memory of MARGARET CHRISTIE wife of WILLIAM ADAM d.2 Feb.1945 aged 76.
(Heart in front) In memory of W. ADAMS (sic) aged 38 also BELLA aged 3½.

-----

5 (Shield) In loving memory of our 2 children. Ever remembered by Mr. & Mrs. RAE.

Erected by MARGARET CRAIG in loving memory of her husband ALEXANDER LEES fisherman
5 Sketraw d.18 May 1896 aged 81. ALEXANDER LEES d.in infancy. Said MARGARET CRAIG d.2
Dec.1903 aged 87; son JOHN d.3 Oct.1919 aged 63.

Erected by CHRISTINA LEES in loving memory of her husband WILLIAM CHRISTIE d.at sea 24
7 Jan.1885 aged 39. Of their family CHRISTINA d.14 May 1882 aged 8; WILLIAM d.22 July 1899
aged 21. Above CHRISTINA LEES d.2 Jan.1933 aged 82. Son-in-law ALEXANDER JOHN ROSS/

447con./McKENZIE fish merchant d.9 Dec.1962 aged 80; ANN his wife d.14 Apr.1966 aged 83.

448   Erected by JAMES CHRISTIE in loving memory of his wife ELIZABETH WOOD d.5 July 1892 aged 30; above JAMES CHRISTIE d.18 Mar.1940 aged 79. His 2nd wife JESSIE ADAM d.12 Apr.1947 aged 80; their dau. JESSIE d.19 Oct.1972 aged 69.

449   Erected to the memory of ALEXANDER son of GEORGE C. ROBERTSON & MARY ANN WALLACE his wife d.28 May 1891 aged 8mths. 1 line motto. (Face now gone)

450   Erected by JAMES MASSON in loving memory of his wife ISABELLA CRUICKSHANK d.Mill of Uras 5 Jan.1924 aged 62; their dau. ANNIE d.22 Jan.1897 aged 2. Above JAMES MASSON d.8 Feb.1939 aged 78.

451   Erected by JOHN WOOD fisherman & MARGARET STEPHEN his wife in loving memory of their son JAMES d.3 Apr.1896 aged 1½; above MARGARET STEPHEN d.8 June 1931 aged 63. HELEN STEPHEN neice (sic) d.10 Feb.1926 aged 26. Above JOHN WOOD d.25 Sept.1939 aged 73; son JAMES d.27 Feb.1963 aged 64.

452   Erected by WILLIAM DUNBAR farmer West Port, Cowie in loving memory of his son FRANCIS JOHN DUNBAR 2/7th Gordon Highlanders d.West Port 28 Mar.1916 aged 22. Said WILLIAM DUNBAR d.there 5 Sept.1929 in 69th year, husband of CHRISTIAN DOUGLAS d.25 Dec.1932 aged 71. 1 line text.

453   Erected by GEORGE DUNBAR in memory of his son GEORGE d.10 Aug.1895 aged 36. Said GEORGE DUNBAR farmer West Port d.23 Sept.1909 aged 73; his wife MARGARET KNOWLES d.25 Nov.1909 aged 72.

454   Sacred to the memory of MARY MARGARET YULE. (no other detail)

455   Erected by a few friends in memory of ALEXANDER MASSIE a native of Banff d.Woodburn Cottage, Muchalls 9 Nov.1889 aged 77. (Now face down)

456   (SUNNY) GEORGE LESLIE THOMSON d.10 Aug.1902. Motto. Plaque on wall behind: VIOLET C.E.C. THOMSON only dau. of GEORGE LESLIE THOMSON & ELIZABETH H.L.THOMSON d.17 May 1968 - interred Broomhill.

457   GEORGE LESLIE THOMSON d.23 Jan.1922. Motto.

458   ELIZABETH HAY LESLIE THOMSON d.3 Nov.1923. Motto.

459   In loving memory of Capt. BRACEY R. WILSON H.B.M.Vice Consul b.14 June 1812 - d.14 Dec. 1889. ELIZABETH LINDSAY his wife d.29 Oct.1921 aged 89.

460   In loving memory of PETER CHRISTIE late of Skateraw d.Bank House, Stonehaven 15 Dec.1916 in 97th year. HELEN CHRISTIE his wife d.Skateraw 15 Jan.1891 in 71st year, dau. of late ANDREW CHRISTIE carpenter Newtonhill. Bottom: Erected by their dau. SUSAN.

461   Erected by JESSIE STEWART in loving memory of her husband JOHN CHRISTIE fisherman Stone haven d.1 Nov.1917 aged 53. Their children ALEXANDRINA, ANDREW, EMY (sic) & LILY d.in infancy. Pte.ALEXANDER CHRISTIE Scottish Rifles d.Ayr County Hospital 22 Oct.1918 aged 21.

2   In loving memory of MARGARET W.G. MASSON wife of HARRY B. ALLAN d.31 Oct.1962 aged 79.

Erected by JOHN MASSON feuer Stonehaven in memory of his .....CHARL..../who...../........./
d.2......./ch......./BE............./d...../JU or JO...../d.1................./ rest gone. (The above stone has now
3   been replaced by the following) In loving memory of MARGARET WALKER GLENNIE wife of
JOHN MASSON shipmaster d.10 Feb.1926 aged 84, a gentle lady. Capt. JOHN MASSON former
Bailie of Stonehaven d.18 Jan.1931 aged 80.

Erected by Mrs McLACHLAN in memory of her mother ISABELLA PATERSON d.8 Oct.1892 aged
4   79. JAMES McLACHLAN draper, her husband d.7 Jan.1912 aged 71. Above Mrs McLACHLAN
d.20 Aug.1921 aged 90. Their nephew JAMES McLACHLAN d.24 Nov.1937 aged 70. R.I.P.

Erected by MARY McPHERSON in memory of her father & mother ROBERT LEES lost at sea
5   1848, MARGARET STEVEN his wife d.Feb.1880 aged 73. Their children GEORGE, ROBERT,
MARGARET & MAY all d.in infancy. JAMES & MURRY (sic) lost at sea.

---

5   (Heart) MARGARET FERRIER aged 56.

---

7   (Heart) JR. RIP.

---

3   In loving memory of GEORGE A. KEITH d.8 Oct.1942.

In loving memory of JOHN THOW d.Coneyhatch 11 May 1891 aged 59; his wife ANN
9   STRACHAN d.1 Feb.1907 aged 73. Son GEORGE d.Royal Inland Hospital, Kamloops, B.C. 23
Oct.1919 aged 58.

Erected by JAMES LOW in loving memory of his wife ISABELLA JAMIESON d.6 Mar.1891 aged
43; his son WILLIAM d.17 July 1895 aged 16. Said JAMES LOW d.8 Nov.1921 aged 77. Here lies
the ashes of GEORGINA HARPER wife of JAMES LOW d.10 Dec.1951 aged 75; JAMES LOW d.3
Apr.1961 aged 90. His eldest son WALTER DENNIS LOW d.6 May 1966 aged 64. Bottom: Also 4
of his children who are interred in the Old Burying Ground.

GS. In memory of GEORGE A. STEPHEN d.29 June 1877 aged 11; MARGARET ANN STEPHEN
d.15 Mar.1879 aged 7. Their mother MARGARET MORRISON d.17 Jan.1890 aged 49;
ALEXANDER STEPHEN d.13 May 1898 aged 32. Space. MARGARET ADAM d.17 Mar.1864
aged 67.

(Book) In memory of WILLIAM CHRISTIE lost at sea 30 May 1890 aged 33; his wife MARGARET
CRAIG d.5 Jan.1906 aged 52. His children JOSEPH d.3 Apr.1890 aged 11mths., DUNCAN C.
MAIN d.30 Dec.1890 aged 5, CHRISTINA d.8 Aug.1901 aged 15.

In loving memory of ALEXANDER FRASER baker d.18 Dec.1909 aged 76; his son JOHN d.6
Apr.1890 aged 17. Wife JEAN CHRISTIE d.1 Sept.1924 aged 77; dau. BARBARA widow of
GEORGE GIBB d.18 Jan.1940 aged 52. Dau. MARGARET d.Aberdeen 4 Nov.1949 aged 66. (Now
face down) (Heart) JOHN FRASER aged 17. 1890.

In loving memory of WILLIAM DICKSON feuar d.Stonehaven 5 Nov.1891 aged 78; his brother
JAMES DICKSON cooper, Royal Navy d.Stonehaven 5 July 1890 aged 76. JANE MORRISON wife
of JAMES DICKSON d.22 Dec.1935 aged 81. Base: 4 lines verse.

475 In loving memory of CHRISTINA TAYLOR wife of ANDREW PATERSON d.30 Aug.1891 aged 31. Their dau. MAGGIE ANN d.14 June 1887 aged 15mths. His 2nd wife ELIZABETH POTTER d.14 Apr.1895 aged 29; above ANDREW PATERSON d.28 Dec.1951 aged 94.

476 Erected by JAMES S. WALKER clothier Newtonhill in memory of his family ISOBELLA SIEVEWRIGHT d.2 Oct.1892 aged 16; JOHN REID d.6 Sept.1893 aged 14; ANNIE REITH d.5 May 1895 aged 10yrs 11mths.; MAGGIE FALCONER d.25 Feb.1896 aged 4. His wife ANNIE REITH d.8 June 1904 aged 48; son JAMES d.6 Oct.1907 aged 29; above JAMES S. WALKER d.8 Jan.1923 aged 73. Bottom: 2 lines text. (Face fragile)

477 RICHARD JOHN WHITTEN Bengal Civil Service (retired) 1841-1918. R.I.P.

478 In loving memory of Capt. JAMES WILLIAM GUY INNES of Raemoir, Royal Navy, CBE, Chev. Legion d'Honneur, D.L. b.Cowie House 11 Sept.1873 - d.Aberdeen 1 Oct.1939. His wife SHEILA b.3 Jan.1878 - d.Aberdeen 12 Mar.1949. 1 line text. Base: 2 lines text.

479 (Plaque on wall) In memory of MICHAEL URQUHART CRUSE 1873-1944 and of his wife MAY WALKER MITCHELL 1872-1933.

480 Erected by EDWARD CRUSE in loving memory of his wife MARIA URQUHART d.Stonehaven 18 July 1900 aged 48; said EDWARD CRUSE for 24 years Town Officer of Stonehaven d.18 Feb.1910 aged 64.

481 In loving memory of FORBES L. REID d.8 Dec.1949 aged 49.

482 (Shield) In loving memory of MARY C. KERR d.in infancy 1935.

483 Erected by ISABELLA CHALMERS in memory of her husband ROBERT CHALMERS d.16 Feb. 1898 aged 35; their son ROBERT d.11 Sept.1897 aged 1yr 8mths.

484 Erected by JAMES DUNCAN Netherley in loving memory of his dau. CHRISTINA d.6 Oct.1897 aged 16; said JAMES DUNCAN d.Stonehaven 1 Oct.1912 aged 82; dau. HELEN ANN d.6 May 1919 aged 54. His wife CATHERINE MILNE d.18 Nov.1920 aged 87; son GEORGE d.Netherley 14 Aug.1954 aged 81.

485 In memory of JOHN COLVIN late sacrist, Aberdeen University d.Stonehaven 2 May 1895 aged 81; ANN THOMSON his wife d.20 Mar.1907 aged 94. ANN SARAH COLVIN their dau. d.Stonehaven 17 Sept.1938 aged 83.

486 In memory of JOHN DAWSON d.5 Sept.1899 aged 75. Erected by his daus. ANN & MARY. (First part now missing)

487 Erected in memory of WILLIAM STOTT d.3 June 1895 aged 90; ANN LEES his wife d.23 Aug. 1859 aged 45. Of their family WILLIAM lost at sea 12 July 1854 aged 20; JEANIE d.1 May 1856 aged 5; ELIZA d.29 Feb.1859 aged 29; ALEXANDER lost at sea 2 Feb.1868 aged 25; GEORGE drowned in River Tyne 23 Nov.1868 aged 22. Of their grandchildren ELIZABETH ROBERTSON ADAMS d.15 Dec.1868 aged 5 weeks; DAVID CHARLES STOTT ADAMS d.Rio de Janeiro 19 May 1894 aged 16. MATTHEW McKAY chief marine engineer d.28 Feb.1954 aged 72, husband of JEAN A.D.ADAMS d.12 Aug.1962 aged 82, dau. of GEORGE ADAMS, husband of ANN STOTT d.Govan 9 June 1906 aged 67; said ANN STOTT d.30 Oct.1925 aged 84.

In loving memory of HENRY GEORGE BAIN d.30 Apr.1894 aged 17; his mother ISABEL EDWARDS d.4 Jan.1910 aged 78.

Erected by GEORGE WOOD in loving memory of his wife JANE MITCHELL d.27 July 1900 aged 67; said GEORGE WOOD d.18 Dec.1906 aged 78. Of their family MARJORY d.12 Aug.1861 aged 5; GEORGE d.18 Sept.1921 aged 67; ANDREW d.7 Feb.1937 aged 78.

In memory of JAMES PIRIE d.22 Sept.1919 aged 55; his wife CHRISTINA CHARLES WOOD d.18 Nov.1929 aged 69. Their son Pte.JAMES PIRIE 6th Gordons killed in action 23 Nov.1917 aged 23; dau. CHRISTINA d.in infancy. MARGARET JANE PIRIE wife of ROBERT MASSON CARNIE d.11 Feb.1949 aged 50 - interred at Warriston, Edinburgh. Bottom: Their grandchild JAMES EDWARD CARNIE d.5 May 1927 aged 7 mths. (Heart) CHRISTINA C. PIRIE aged 1mth.

MARY GRANT wife of GEORGE SORRIE teacher b.Abernethy 8 Mar.1850 - d.Stonehaven 1 Apr. 1893. GEORGE SORRIE M.A. headmaster Stonehaven Public School b.Kintore 4 Dec.1854 - d.Stonehaven 14 June 1921. MARY GRANT M.A. their eldest dau. b.Abernethy 7 Oct.1877 - d.Wolverhampton 6 May 1925. GEORGE SORRIE M.A., B.L. their elder son b.Abernethy 27 Mar. 1879 - d.Glasgow 30 Mar.1932. ISABEL SORRIE or HALLER d.19 Mar.1960.

In loving memory of my grand uncle WILLIAM TAYLOR d.18 July 1895 aged 66; his father JAMES TAYLOR d.28 Feb.1843 aged 61, his mother CHRISTINA LEES d.12 Feb.1862 aged 79 also his 2 brothers JAMES d.8 Mar.1831 aged 19, ANDREW d.7 Aug.1830 aged 13. My uncle JOHN MIDDLETON d.23 Jan.1893 aged 56, my grandmother (not named) d.12 May 1894 aged 93. My brother WILLIAM LEES MIDDLETON d.3 June 1895 aged 18; my father WILLIAM GORDON MIDDLETON d.17 Oct.1907 aged 65. My mother CHRISTINA LEES d.1 Nov.1913 aged 63. Erected by HELEN ELLIS.

In memory of JAMES ELLIS tailor d.Detroit, USA 21 Mar.1911 aged 40 - interred in Elmwood Cemetery. HELEN MIDDLETON his wife d.31 Jan.1929 aged 54 and of their family JOHN MOIR ELLIS d.5 Sept.1917 aged 13.

(Heart) GEORGE McGREGOR aged 8mths. 1894.

In loving memory of GEORGE McGERGOR Cowie Mills d.Cowie Cottage 31 July 1917 aged 77; his sons GEORGE d.Mill of Uras 29 Jan.1908 aged 38; JOHN SILVER killed in action in France 11 May 1917 aged 36; DAVID d.8 Dec.1929 aged 53. His wife ELIZA TURRIFF d.19 June 1936 aged 89; his dau. FLORA d.23 Jan.1938 aged 52.

(Shield) ANNIE McGREGOR 6 years.

(Shield) JAMES G. BAIN aged 18 mths. 1896.

In loving memory of JAMES BAIN farmer Cairneywhin d.19 Aug.1922 aged 52; sons JAMES d.Oldcake aged 18mths.; HERBERT d.of wounds in France 10 Sept.1918 aged 30.

Erected by ALEXANDER CHRISTIE fisherman Torry & ELSPET LEES his wife in loving memory of their sons ALEXANDER d.14 Oct.1894 aged 13; JAMES d.25 Feb.1903 aged 7yrs 9mths. Above ALEXANDER CHRISTIE d.25 Oct.1939 aged 84. Also GEORGE aged 51 & GEORGE HOLMES son-in-law aged 48 both lost at sea Mar.1941. ELSPET LEES his wife d.4 Dec.1944 aged 86; their dau. ELSPET JANE widow of GEORGE HOLMES d.30 July 1980 aged 88.

500   Erected by WILLIAM & JANE CHRISTIE Torry in loving memory of their family JANE d.19 Mar. 1894 aged 1yr 8mths.; JOHN d.18 May 1924 aged 28. Above JANE CHRISTIE d.8 Dec.1935 aged 73; above WILLIAM CHRISTIE d.25 Jan.1940 aged 77..

---

501   Erected by WILLIAM GALLAGHER clothier Stonehaven in memory of ANNIE DUNCAN GOVE his wife d.21 June 1894 aged 33. Family: MAGGIE, MARY, ANNIE, RUTH & LIZZIE all d.in infancy; KATIE d.26 May 1894 aged 8; WILLIE d.20 July 1894 aged 3. Above WILLIAM GALLAGHER d.7 Apr.1919 aged 62. (RHS) In memory of his father HUGH GALLAGHER b.County Donegal, Ireland 1826 d.17 May 1870; his brother & sisters JOHN d.12 Nov.1871 aged 13; MARY d.25 July 1888 aged 21; LIZZIE d.12 Nov.1888 aged 18. His mother CATHERINE ANDERSON d.17 July 1908 aged 79. Base: Brother HUGH saddler Montrose d.28 Mar.1901 aged 47 - interred in Sleepyhillock Cemetery. (LHS) ISABELLA MATHIESON wife of said WILLIAM GALLAGHER d.17 June 1934 aged 80.

---

502   In loving memory of WILLIAM CHRISTIE fisherman Cowie d.13 Aug.1892 aged 71; his wife ISOBEL CHRISTIE d.2 Jan.1899 aged 77. Their youngest son WILLIAM fisherman d.24 Jan.1944 aged 77; his wife SUSAN MASSON d.8 Apr.1959 aged 87. Son WILLIAM d.27 Sept.1979 aged 76; his wife JEAN McARA MILLER d.8 Apr.1984 aged 84. And ELIZABETH CHRISTIE dau. of the above WILLIAM & SUSAN CHRISTIE d.17 July 1997 aged 91. (Heart) JANE CHRISTIE aged 1yr 8mths.

---

503   Erected in memory of Pte. JAMES R. CHRISTIE 2nd Seaforth Highlanders missing 27 Mar.1918 aged 21. His mother MARY LEES d.12 June 1938 aged 79; his father JOHN CHRISTIE d.4 July 1942 aged 87. Sister JESSIE d.10 June 1958 aged 68.

---

504   In loving memory of HELEN ISOBEL D. CHRISTIE d.18 June 1962 aged 30; her mother MARGARET F.S.CHRISTIE d.21 Sept.1983 aged 84.

---

505   Erected by JAMES CHRISTIE cooper in loving memory of his family WILLIAM ALEXANDER d.28 Feb.1878 aged 15mths.; JOHN d.13 Apr.1903 aged 13; ALEXANDER EDWARD d.(the result of an accident) 17 May 1910 aged 30; JAMES EDWARD d.Elizabethville, Congo 26 Feb.1911 aged 32; WILLIAM, R.N.Division d.France 18 June 1917 aged 33. Above JAMES CHRISTIE d.17 Feb. 1937 aged 80; his wife MARJORY EDWARD d.5 June 1938 aged 82.

---

506   ANTHONY STEWART NORMAN infant son of PHYLLIS & JOHN NORMAN 25 June 1947.

---

507   In memory of Mrs. ELIZABETH HENDERSON widow of GEORGE HENDERSON b.2 Nov.1846 d.Cowie House 15 Mar.1895. A loving nurse to little children. Base: 3 lines text.

---

508   ALEXANDER INNES of Cowie 1892-1975. His wife ALBERTA LAURA INNES 1890-1975.

---

509   2 lines verse. HELEN AMY wife of WILLIAM DISNEY INNES of Cowie b.18 July 1858 - d.8 Apr. 1892. Above Rev. WM. DISNEY INNES b.17 Oct.1851 - d.31 Oct.1928.

Abercrombie:- 56.
Abercromby:- 164.
Aberdein:- 25.
Abernethie:- 122
Abernethy:- 124.
Adam:- 138,183,185,186,224,231,299,301,
312,313,327,366,439,443,444,448,471.
Adams:- 139,140,187,314,418,444,487.
Airth:- 85.
Allan:- 17,145,337,462.
Allardyce:- 215,401.
Anderson:- 35,313,330,331,415,501.
Angus:- 131,305,306,307,308.
Archibald:- 393,403.
Arcari:- 402.
Arthur:- 271.
Ashmore:- 378.

Bain:- 75,121,138,336,337,352,488,497,498.
Barclay:- 160,215,420,421,422.
Barrack:- 235.
Barrie:- 404.
Bayly:- 1.
Beattie:- 4,310.
Beith:- 405.
Berry:- 307.
Bettie:- 180.
Beverly:- 61,63.
Bisset:- 42,76,227.
Bissot:- 63.
Black:- 36.
Blair:- 179,205,217,230,237,408.
Boaden:- 103.
Boniface:- 216.
Bowman:- 404.
Brebner:- 17,242.
Bridgeford:- 361.
Brodie:- 48,50,136,163,168,208,209,210,
211,213,251,298.
Brown:- 36,40,51,52,53,54,56,57,58,59,60,
61,62,63,97,112,113,277,371.
Browne:- 176.
Bruce:- 306.
Buchan:- 4,5.
Burnes:- 61.
Burnet:- 156,188,191,192,196,240,247,262,
292,323.
Burnett:- 8,30,160,244,263,328.

Cadenhead:- 253,352,397.
Cadonhead:- 171.

Caddonhead:- 204.
Caie:- 169.
Caird:- 68,178,262,375.
Calder:- 171,204,434.
Callder:- 183.
Cameron:- 390.
Carnegie:- 248,362,366,367,426.
Carneggie:- 194.
Carnegy:- 130.
Carnie:- 490.
Chalmers:- 41,64,133,194,342,343,379,392,393,
483.
Chapman:- 435.
Charles:- 363,368,490.
Christe:- 151.
Christie:- 14,23,33,43,44,47,48,50,55,71,79,83,95,
96,98,100,117,123,125,127,134,135,136,
140,145,150,152,161,162,163,172,173,179,
182,184,185,186,197,201,206,208,214,218,
220,226,228,238,239,243,246,248,250,251,
252,257,258,259,260,261,266,270,278,279,
280,281,282,283,284,285,286,287,290,291,
293,296,298,300,304,319,321,328,329,338,
348,378,387,408,412,416,429,432,436,438,
444,447,448,460,461,472,473,499,500,502,
503,504,505.
Clanachan:- 405.
Clark:- 139,234.
Cobb:- 396.
Cocher:- 317.
Cocke:- 192.
Collie:- 4,26,334,414.
Collison:- 196.
Colvin:- 485.
Cook:- 111.
Cormack:- 260.
Cormie:- 393.
Cormock:- 344.
Court:- 216.
Coutts:- 69.
Cowie:- 177,278.
Craib:- 413.
Craig:- 47,99,117,149,209,243,287,300,310,311,
395,416,429,441,446,472.
Crichton:- 407.
Criggie:- 233.
Cromar:- 137.
Crowley:- 370,371,372.
Cruickshank:- 306,450.
Cruse:- 479,480.
Crystie:- 86.

COWIE, MAIN INDEX

Morrison:- 471,474.

Morton:- 265.

Mouat:- 68,221..

Mowat:- 324.

Muir:- 276.

Munro:- 266.

Murdoch:- 400,404.

Murison:- 81.

Murray:- 142,226,334,350,374,391.

Nairn:- 265.

Napier:- 121,122,148,155,298.

Neiper:- 3.

Neper:- 92,104,347.

Newdick:- 270.

Nicolson:- 105,106.

Noble:- 173,424.

Norman:- 506.

Ogg:- 238,239.

O'Harrow:- 174.

Orchie:- 124.

Osborne:- 420.

Pargiter:- 108.

Paterson:- 75,76,77,79,274,464,475.

Perrin:- 215.

Pirie:- 490.

Pithie:- 13,34,134.

Porter:- 397.

Potter:- 475.

Powell:- 420.

Proctor:- 385.

Pyper:- 13,73.

Rae:- 445.

Ramsden:- 268.

Rea:- 269.

Reid:- 62,94,105,203,440a,476,481.

Reith:- 250,330,421,476.

Rickards:- 108.

Riddell:- 437.

Ritchie:- 147,217,305,308.

Robb:- 333,337.

Robert:- 115.

Roberts:- 116.

Robertson:- 18,38,39,42,80,81,108,126,135,
137,345,377,449,487.

Rose:- 216.

Ross:- 447.

Russel:- 442.

Russell:- 268.

Sadlyor:- 315.

Sawer:- 398.

Scorgie:- 327.

Scott:- 38,375,377.

Search:- 437.

Seaton:- 349.

Sharpe:- 375.

Shepherd:- 389.

Sheret:- 332.

Shewan:- 435.

Sievewright:- 476.

Silver:- 495.

Sim:- 16,21.

Simpson:- 73,255,328.

Smart:- 264,265.

Smith:- 65,84,85,153,268,364,367.

Smyth:- 384.

Sorrie:- 491.

Souter:- 177.

Souttar:- 373,376,383.

Spark:- 6,7,8,9,10,11,12,26,27,58,73,334,357,
358,377.

Spence:- 194.

Stephen:- 151,153,167,168,169,170,256,297,303,
380,392,399,451,471.

Steven:- 465.

Stewart:- 129,238,382,461,506.

Stott:- 19,362,426,487.

Strachan:- 115,116,118,147,238,242,244,330,331,
351,434,469.

Strathdee:- 13.

Sutherland:- 345.

Tait:- 116.

Tawse:- 215.

Taylor:- 15,52,62,88,89,91,93,98,100,101,102,130,
138,141,147,148,164,214,235,252,363,386,
388,391,394,409,475,492.

Tester:- 249.

Thom:- 156,157,424.

Thomson:- 18,21,38,52,54,180,191,223,456,457,
458,485.

Thow:- 469.

Tindal:- 302.

Tomper:- 241.

Troup:- 221.

Turriff:- 21,495.

Urquhart:- 479,480.

Alexander:- 150,152,153,172,235,237,251,
255,284,322,328,427,428,446.
Ann:- 88,251,487.
Andrew:- 33,153,215,232,235,237,245,246,
303,322.
Arthur Wellesley Kinnear:- 235.

Charles:- 233,255,428.
Christian:- 200.
Christina:- 32,83,256,329,439,447,492.
Constance:- 428.

Elizabeth:- 304.
Elspet:- 149,297,416,499.

Fredrick:- 235.

George:- 145,149,153,303,304,322,441,465.

Helen:- 83,226.

Isabella:- 198,237,251,256.

James:- 40,,95,255,256,266,322,328,427,
428,465.
James Burnett:- 328.
Jane:- 153,205,233,307,316,322,427,465.
Jane Ann Fyfe:- 328

Jane Christie:- 266.
Jane Dickson:- 235.
Jean:- 153,303.
Jessie Matilda:- 215.
John:- 153,232,237,255,328,446.

Maggie Jane:- 304.
Margaret:- 45,71,145,149,150,162,172,235,243,
245,255,260,266,465.
Margret:- 153,255.
Mary:- 153,503.
Mary Anabella:- 328.
Mary Ann:- 434.
May:- 465.
Murry:- 465.

Peter:- 152,167,246.

Ritchie:- 233.
Robert:- 145,231,232,233,237,255,328,465.
Robert Simpson:- 255.

Susan:- 236.

Thomas:- 33.

William:- 152,153,232,233,234,284,294,304.

Cowie, Extended Index - MASSON

Alexander:- 132,200,286,290,297,338,348.
Andrew:- 73,74,198,200,202,203,293,338.
Ann:- 44,74,213,298.
Annie:- 450.

Barbara:- 200.

Christian:- 202,283,291.
Christina:- 73,339,436.

Elizabeth:- 43,201,203,285,297.
Elsie:- 132.
Elspet:- 338.
Elspeth:- 291.
Elspith:- 300.

George:- 73,198,296,298.

Helen:- 132,245,290,294,440.

Isabella:- 43,189,198,279,290,293,438.
Isobel:- 182,298,338.

James:- 43,72, 203,286,291,297,298,299,318,
  338,450.
Jane:- 20,202,282,285,298.
Janet:- 37,243,261,295.
Jannet:- 295.
Jean:- 72,246,290,291.
Jessie:- 198.
John:- 43,200,202,295,298,300,318,463.
Joseph:- 72,78.

Margaret:- 76,211,257,290,291,293,296,298,338.
Margaret May:- 203.
Margaret W.G.:- 462.
Margrat:- 104.
Mary:- 125,232,287,321,338.
Mary Jane:- 100.

Robert:- 32,132,198,201,290.

Susan:- 502.
Susanna:- 286.

William:- 72,73,132,203,297,300.